A Century
of Spells

A Century of Spells

Draja Mickaharic

SAMUEL WEISER, INC.
York Beach, Maine

First published in 1988 by
Samuel Weiser, Inc.
Box 612
York Beach, Maine 03910

Library of Congress Cataloging-in-Publication Data

Mickaharic, Draja.
    A century of spells / Draja Mickaharic.
        p.   cm.
    Includes index.
    ISBN 0-87728-647-7
    1. Incantations.   2. Magic.   I. Title.
    BF1558.M53   1988   88-3962
    133.4′4--dc19   CIP

Typeset in 10 point Century Schoolbook
Printed in the United States of America

Painting on the front cover is from a private collection and is
used by kind permission of the owner.

CONTENTS

Omnisciently
humanity requires
so simple a task
as to fulfill desires

Man is created to praise, reverence and serve God our Lord, and by this means to save his soul. All other things on the face of the earth are created for man to help him fulfil the end for which he is created. From this it follows that man is to use these things to the extent that they will help him to attain his end. Likewise he must rid himself of them as so far as they prevent him from attaining it.

St. Ignatius Loyola
*The Spiritual Exercises**

*Garden City, NY: Doubleday, 1964, p. 47.

Therefore I say to you,
Anything you pray for and ask,
Believe that you will receive it,
And it will be done for you.
And when you stand up to pray,
Forgive what you have against any man,
So that your Father in heaven will forgive
    you your trespasses,
But if you will not forgive,
Even your Father in heaven will not forgive
    you your trespasses.

Mark 11: 24–26

For you God subjected all that is in
    the heavens
And on earth, all from Him.
Behold! In that are signs for people
    who reflect.

Koran 45:18

A Caution to the inexperienced in this ART, and a Word of Advice to those who would be Adepts.

Brother,

It is necessary for me to inform thee, that whatever thy desires are in the pursuit of this art, which we call Magic, so wilt thy connection and answer be. If in the pursuit of revenge, it is but proper thou shouldest know that thou wilt, in any of these experiments here laid down, draw to thyself a revengeful demon, or an infernal furious spirit, serving in the principle of the wrath of God; if worldly riches and aggrandizement, then thou shalt have an earthial or fiery spirit, which will delude thee with the riches of the central world; if fame, or the blaze of glory, then the spirit of pride will be allotted to thee, who will gratify thy inordinate desire of vain glory; for all these offices are there spirits allotted and will be eagar to mix with thy spirit: it will attract thee to his own nature, and serve all thy purposes according to the extent of God's permission; and as thy desires are and from what principal they proceed, so shalt thou be answered: but if thou desirest to know nothing but for the honor and glory of God, and the help of thy neighbor, and, in great humility, fill thy heart with the love of God, thou shalt then have a pure spirit which will grant (by the Lord's permission) they desires. Therefore seek for that which is good; avoid all evil either in thought word or action; pray to God to fill thee with wisdom, and thou shalt reap an abundant harvest. There are two ways magically set before thee; chuse which thou wilt, thou shalt be sure of thy reward. Farewel.

London 1800   Francis Barrett*

---

*From *The Magus* pp. 134–135. Available from Citadel Press, Secaucus, NJ.

INTRODUCTION

This book is a practical introduction to natural magic. It may be considered a textbook, or, better, a workbook. You can learn natural magic from working through this book as much as it is possible to learn magic from any text. The book is also intended to be useful as a reference work for the practicing magician.

This book contains examples of many different types of spells, along with examples of spells from a number of different magical practices. It will give you an overview of the field of natural magic so you can decide whether or not you wish to pursue the study of magic. At all times, my intent has been to clearly explain the advantages and limitations of the magical art.

The development of magical abilities is the result of the spiritualization of the human soul. The closer we grow to our creator, the greater are our abilities and perceptions of the divine reality. It is this divine reality that is the true reality our physical universe imperfectly reflects.

Those who have refined their senses by harmonizing them with the divine reality can see interconnections between otherwise unrelated things. The ability to sense this interconnection forms the basis for all magical operations. Those who are true adepts have developed their moral and ethical senses along with their magical powers. They do not display their abilities randomly or in a negative manner.

Judaism, Christianity and Islam all recognize that humankind has been granted dominion over the things of the earth by our creator. Psalm 8, verses 4 through 6, is an excellent testimony for this concept. This is a real dominion, freely given by God to all who are able to take advantage of it. It is another foundation of natural magic.

Because true priests or priestesses have achieved a harmony with the divine reality of the creator, they are able to demonstrate their dominion over creation. Being able to demonstrate this dominion is what separates the true priest or priestess from the false.

True magic always has a physical result on the earth. It does not end in dreams, delusions, and self-deception. True magic is a natural ability that is developed as a result of spiritual growth. It is never the product of a search for power or privilege.

It is wise to keep this in mind as you read this book.

Draja Mickaharic

PUBLISHER'S NOTE

Nothing in this book will heal a physical condition, or in any way replace the skill and experience of a medical practitioner. Consult your physician for physical illnesses. This work is concerned only with spiritual conditions.

Deviating from the instructions given in this book may be harmful, and could even cause serious damage to the spiritual nature of the experimenter. The baths mentioned herein are for external use only and could cause physical harm if taken internally. Because some of the following spells may sound "simple" and interesting, don't get the idea to "do a variation." When you try to work magic using only your own enthusiasm you are treading in dangerous waters. Follow the directions as they are presented here. The publisher and author assume no liability for personal harm that may result from any deviation from the instructions.

1 *Protection Spells*

In our normal everyday lives we are influenced – mentally and emotionally – by many things. We absorb and shed these influences, giving them no thought. As we enter into the study of magic and the occult we lose the protection that our ignorance provides. We may also begin to expose ourselves to people who may not be particularly well disposed toward us. We need to learn to protect ourselves as our awareness of the divine reality gradually increases.

There are a number of ways by which we are influenced by others. The most obvious way is through conversation. And we are all aware of advertising and that it influences us. But how many of us are really *conscious* of the effects of advertising and persuasion in our daily lives? When we are not aware of how we are influenced by something that is so apparent in our lives, is it any surprise to find that we completely ignore the more subtle influences which daily impinge upon us?

Human beings exist mentally and emotionally as well as physically. When we are influenced, either by another person or by an advertising campaign, we are responding to conscious mental influence. When we are influenced by another person (or by a group of other people) to behave in an uncharacteristic way, we are usually responding to subconscious mental influences. For example, how many times have you "gone with the group" to another bar when you really just wanted to go home?

Cheering wildly at a sporting event is an obvious case of conscious emotional response. But feeling sad or lonely without apparent cause is an example of subconscious emotional response—in this case we are feeling and displaying an emotion, but we are not consciously aware of *why*.

Once we become consciously aware of the various parts of our being, we are able to understand how we are being influenced, and whether we are being influenced by another person. While working toward the goal of conscious awareness, we should follow a regular program of self-protection and spiritual cleansing. This will serve to assist us in our development while keeping the influences of our daily lives away from us.

You should familiarize yourself with two books that provide information regarding the process of spiritual cleansing and psychic protection, *Spiritual Cleansing* and *Psychic Self Defense*.[1] Follow the program for spiritual cleansing given on page 91 of *Spiritual Cleansing*. This will protect you as you open yourself to a greater awareness of the divine reality.

There are two basic kinds of protection you can learn. The most important is a passive type, and involves protecting yourself against the influences that come from life in general. The second type is the reversal of spells, or "work," consciously sent to you from someone else. In this chapter we will discuss the more passive forms of protection. In the next chapter we will discuss reversing spells and negative magic.

---

[1] See *Psychic Self Defense* by Dion Fortune (Wellingborough, England: Thorsons Publishing Group, 1977) available in the USA from Samuel Weiser, Inc.; and *Spiritual Cleansing* by Draja Mickaharic (York Beach, ME: Samuel Weiser, 1982).

The magician's primary instrument is him- or herself. The development of your own natural abilities is the first step in any form of magical training. This is a process that begins with the repetitive practice of certain exercises. It also involves understanding certain things through self-observation. The information I am giving you here is the same information I was given by my first teacher many years ago. While it may seem very introductory, even childishly simple, it must be followed through to obtain success.

Throughout the course of each day you are surrounded by the forces of the divine creation. Some of these forces are visible, in that they impact upon your senses. We see the brightness of the sun, or the haze of an overcast day. We can hear and feel the wind in either gentle gusts or gales. We can feel and smell the rain and the earth. Other forces of the divine creation are invisible, in that they do not impact upon our senses. We cannot physically sense the motions and interrelationships of the planets in the heavens or the energies radiated by those around us, but we are influenced by them nonetheless.

The sum total of the forces of the divine creation manifest themselves in each of us individually. They manifest themselves in the flux of our emotions or changes in our mental states. The fact that our emotions fluctuate inexplicably, or that our mental states change from moment to moment, is an indication that neither relates to our real personality.

One of the first principles to understand in any occult study is that you are not just mind or emotion. This is a basic tenet of any religious practice, whether you study Christianity, Judaism, Hinduism, Islam, Buddhism, or whatever. It is also a very difficult concept for most people to accept.

Once we are able to observe ourselves, we can sense those conscious influences much as we sense the physical presence of wind, rain and sunlight. The attempts of others to sway us mentally are brought out clearly and we see them for what they are. Subconscious influence we can sense emotionally. We can *feel* it — and know that it has a quality that differentiates it from fear, apprehension or the emotional blockage of inhibition.

Once we are able to sense these influences upon us, we will realize two important things: first, they cannot harm our true essence; and second, our accepting these influences into the self is our own conscious choice. We can deny others any influence over us.

This is obviously not something that we can do initially. It is a state that we must develop. We develop this state through conscious effort.

It is necessary that you develop a base within yourself – a base that is not affected by your changing surface emotions or your changing mental states. This base must become a point of contact for your real personality, the essence of the divine which is within you and within everyone else. From this base you can reach out to know your emotions or to quiet your mind. This base, once established, gradually becomes a place of stability, allowing you to develop an internal awareness that cannot be disturbed by influences from any external source.

The development of this internal base takes a great deal of time – years, actually. Once this base is developed it will pay great dividends in terms of personal development. Obviously, some of you will find your internal base more quickly than others. This development cannot be left to chance, nor can you assume that it is naturally present. This base is brought into being only through concerted effort. The easiest way to develop your base is through the daily practice of the following exercise: For half an hour every day relax your body. Relax by letting all of the tension out of your muscles. Allow your mind to run free, without paying the least attention to any thoughts that may enter it. Do this as part of your daily routine until it becomes second nature to you.

By using this exercise you will eventually begin to understand that there is more to you than just your body, emotions and mind. This may start as an intellectual understanding, but it will become a deep inexpressible truth. When you contact this part of yourself, focus your attention on it when you are in a relaxed state. Gradually you will find it possible to contact it in your normal waking state. Gradually allow this part of yourself to enter your daily life. Direct your attention to it whenever you are able to do so during the day and you will discover that it can guide you. If you follow the guidance it gives, you will discover that it can become an active participant in your life, and it can make your life easier in many ways. This part of you is the true eternal you. You may commune with that part of yourself on a daily basis, casting off all the influences which may come to you during the day. After you practice this for some time you will find that you no longer accept external influences and you have actually begun acting in harmony with your true personality.

If you have any religious practice, regardless of what it is, you should make a daily routine of praying. Every religious practice has its regular prayers, and these should be made a part of your daily routine as well. If you have no religious practice you should return to the religious practice of your childhood, and enter into it with new perception that it is actually valuable and worthwhile. If you grew up in a home with no religious practice, you should look around and find one that is comfortable for you. Enter into the practice and use the prayers from that practice. If the practice uses prayers in a foreign language, you should learn the language, at least well enough to understand the prayers.

Popular opinion to the contrary, it really doesn't matter which prayers you use or what form they take. What matters is whether or not you pray regularly. Prayer (and the attempt at praying) acts to stabilize and keep you protected from various forms of external influence.

True prayer is the most magical act there is, and if you are in communion with the divine, you live your life in a state of continual prayer. Prayer is a real force in the universe, and the process of learning how to pray is one of the most important lessons you can learn.

If you want to take a more active part in protecting yourself from conscious influence, you can learn to close your aura. You can close off your aura deliberately and willfully to prohibit external influences from impinging on it. Men who regularly wear belts may do this by using the buckling of the belt as a deliberate action that seals them off from any external influences. People who do not regularly wear belts may close themselves off by obtaining a length of small cotton cord about a foot longer than their waist measurement. Tie the cord around your waist as you dress in the morning. This becomes a deliberate act (or ritual) to protect yourself from external influences and the ritual will seal you off. The cord should be tied around the waist and worn under your clothes.

You may also seal your aura through the process of a regular morning and evening prayer. Any number of prayers have the effect of limiting the kinds of influences which you accept during the course of the day. Any prayer may be used for this purpose, including a prayer of your own devising. The following prayer is typical of those which may be employed for this purpose:

> The Lord surrounds me with light, love and protection. I am safe within this sphere of love from all which may seek to harm me.

Your own belief that you are protected is one of the most important factors in any form of protection. The stronger and more certain your belief, the more you are protected from external influence.

The effect (either intentionally, or as a secondary effect) of many spiritual exercises given to students is the removal of many external influences which have affected them. These influences are both conscious and sub-conscious, and they must be removed in order for the students to progress on their paths. For example, *The Spiritual Exercises* of St. Ignatius Loyola have this result.[2]

People committed to a program of spiritual development find they are no longer subject to the types of influence which formerly afflicted them. Eventually, as the students develop, they are no longer subject to any external influence whatsoever. This is a rare achievement, for it means that they are no longer suggestible in any way. To limit suggestibility is one of the goals of our evolution. Like everything else in the development of the soul, it is reached by one person at a time.

---

[2]Image Books, Doubleday & Co., Garden City, NY, 1964.

2 *Reversing Spells*

Almost all the popular spell books, books about candle-burning or praying for magical purposes have the primary goal of influencing another person. Fortunately most people who are initiated into the practice of magic have a highly developed sense of morality and are not interested in controlling others. However, this chapter is devoted to keeping yourself free of the magicians who don't feel that way.

When you try to influence another person, for good or for ill, you are in some sense practicing a form of black magic. The black magician attempts to influence the subconscious of another person by changing his or her behavior, action, or emotional response. So all the curses, love spells, and spells to make debtors pay are forms of black magic. Black magic can induce feelings of hate or guilt, and high-pressure selling or emotionally oriented advertising is considered a form of it. Obviously there are many varieties and degrees of black magic – some forms are more negative than others – yet all are attempts to influence a decision of some sort.

Any form of black magic involves *karma*. It is known as a form of "moral malpractice" and will be paid back as karma in a future existence. The concept that we need to understand is simple – eventually the soul will learn not to attempt to influence others. At the present stage of human development, however, many people decide that magic might as well be used to attain the ends they desire. This chapter is devoted to reversing the spells that may be sent your way by a student magician, or an individual who has studied magic to gain power over others.

It is a relatively simple matter to break a curse, and I will show you how to do this with ease. But before we go into the reversing procedures, it is important to understand a little of what you may need to look for aside from knowing how to reverse a spell.

Many people who think they have been cursed are suffering not from a curse, but from a lack of self-importance. People who are mentally unbalanced, people who want to be powerful and important, sometimes think they have been cursed. And the curse itself gives them a feeling of importance. So you may do a reversing spell for someone who has convinced you that he or she is under some terrible influence, and when you have done the reverse work nothing changes. Which means that the person wasn't under any spell except the spell of self-delusion. That condition needs a cure, too, and if you are a spiritual practitioner, you will learn to redirect the individual in a direction that would be more beneficial.

As you continue to study magic your senses will become more tuned, and your intuition and awareness level will spot certain conditions in people that you may not have noticed before. For example, you may see someone that you know who is obviously under some kind of a spell, but the individual doesn't know it. When you try to say something to this person, he or she makes it clear that the change is one that he or she made on a voluntary basis. In this situation, you can do nothing. But you may be curious to understand how someone could change drastically and not be aware of what happened. Well, the human mind is a wonderful mechanism! The rational mind can explain any situation it finds itself in, and even the youngest child can provide a reasonable explanation as to why he or she did something. This process of self-justification—which exists uncontrolled in almost everyone—rationalizes any changes in behavior very easily, and can even convince us that the change is desirable.

Some people may think they have been cursed, and it's a good idea to ask if they have been to a store-front psychic or fortune teller. Store-front psychics make money by telling their clients that they are cursed. Then the client pays the store-front psychic to take the curse away. Innocent people sometimes really believe this, and may come to you to have a curse removed. Before removing it, make sure it's there. The chances are that the person has no curse at all. Making money by fibbing about being cursed or under a spell brings its share of karma to the practitioner.

The most common curse that might have to be broken is the petty curse set up by amateur magicians. Here, the student learns a ritual and it is successful, and this one success convinces him (or her) that he has great magical ability. This causes two kinds of problems. First, the student enters the realm of fantasy and thinks he has absolute control over his life and the lives of others through acts of magic. He rationalizes every failure and can actually block sensory awareness if the physical world doesn't correspond to the world of fantasy that he lives in. Magicians, or would-be magicians, of this caliber enter into a world of delusion and self-deception. They may continue to function in the real world to some extent, but there is a tendency to exert influence upon themselves which further encourages self-deception and delusion. Obviously this is an unproductive way to live.

The student who has suddenly gained great magical powers may exert love spells, or other power spells on people he knows. If you attend a class, or go to a place where magicians meet, you may run into someone who will try to place a spell on you to test his or her power. This is idiotic, but it is done. And that is why you need to know how to reverse a spell, so you don't waste time in your own development by being de-energized by amateur power-seekers.

True curses are rare. There are not that many magicians who are powerful enough to really perform black magic. In order to develop magical power, the animal instinctual nature has to be placed under control. Few people interested in the concept of black magic are willing to put the necessary work into preparation for study. When the instinctual nature is uncontrolled, it tends to accept credit for any successful performance of any magical act, and that acceptance acts as a block so that further magical operations are brought to a halt.

Serious students of magic – who have really developed their magical ability to the point where they could really influence others – don't waste their time on negative spell-casting. The study of magic is really a course in self-development of a particular nature. When you start considering the evolution of the soul, who cares about whether or not you can make "Mary" love you?

Now that we've discussed all the reasons why someone is probably not cursed in the first place, let's move on to reversing negative spells. The whole process of trying to determine who has cast a spell or curse is a waste of time. It really doesn't make any difference who did the work, the only important thing is that it is removed. Replying to a curse with a curse will only be an escalating factor in a war, and students who do this get caught in a magical-curse syndrome that may end up making them paranoid. Turn from the curse and break it, and let it go. Thank God it's gone, and don't look for negative effects around the one who you think has cast it.

The following spells are excellent cursebreakers. They act to return curses and influence to their source. If no curse has been sent, the cursebreakers do not return to you or to the one who has used it.

REVERSING A SPELL WITH WATER

The water method of reversing a spell is particularly effective for spells which were originally cast with water, or spells geared to affect the emotions. This method is an excellent way to rid yourself of love spells in any of their many forms. You should perform the spell yourself if you have been the victim. If you want to help others to reverse a spell, remember that the spell should be reversed by the actual victim.

Fill a small bottle with water. You can use a baby food jar, or a jar of similar size. Place at least a dozen straight pins in the bottle. Cap the bottle tightly and place it over a fire. The bottle may be placed on the kitchen stove. The bottle is heated until it explodes, which casts the pins all over the room. The pins and the broken glass should be cleaned up and placed in the garbage. Remove the garbage from the house immediately. The clean-up must be done as soon as possible after the bottle explodes.

The purpose of this spell is to disturb the negative influences of the water element that are present in the home of the victim. This spell reverses any negative work, and attempts to restore balance to the "water element" presence in the victim's home. This is a very effective spell, and has been taught by practitioners of three different practices. I have used it with success several times.

The bottle used may be of any size, although a baby food jar or a small jam jar is probably best suited for the spell because this type of jar only holds a few ounces of liquid. Ordinary tap water is used in the spell, and the steel pins used by dressmakers are fine. They should be placed loose in the bottle, after the water has been added to the bottle. You can use as many pins as you like, but you should use at least a dozen.

Heat the bottle when no one is in the room. It's very important that no one should be in the room when the bottle explodes, for one may be hurt by flying glass or pins. The smaller the bottle, the faster it will heat, another reason for using a small jar. When the bottle is hot enough it will explode, strewing the pins and broken glass, as well as water, all over the room. The purpose of immediately cleaning up the mess is to remove the influence of the spell immediately. Once the influence is out of the house it is very difficult for the person who did the work to re-establish the connection to the house.

REVERSING A SPELL WITH FIRE

This method of reversing a spell is particularly effective for magical work that has been done with fire. This covers the entire range of candle magic, as well as any magic intended to influence your thoughts. Some people may want to use this spell on a regular basis at the full moon, for it will provide protection against all of the usual negative influences from others which accumulate in the course of a month. You will need a coffee cup full of dirt and a candle to use this spell. City dwellers who do not have access to dirt in their backyards may use potting soil. You can use any kind of candle.

Take a small candle (such as a birthday candle) and light it. Place it in dirt (in the coffee cup) while it is lit and allow the flame to stabilize. With a sudden motion, take the candle from the dirt and reverse it, extinguishing the lit end in the dirt. Bite the burned end off the candle and light it again, saying:

As the candle flame is reversed, so let all that opposes
me be reversed. As the flame has perished in the dirt,
let those who oppose me come to nothing in their work.

The candle is now left to burn out. When it burns out, put the candle and the dirt in the garbage and remove it from your home.

This spell comes from Brazil, where it has been used successfully for many years. It has been considered an effective curse-breaker. If a curse is actually present, this spell often produces an immediately feeling of relief as soon as the prayer has been said. In some cases the relief can be impressive, as the spell may be done by one person for another. However, when this spell is done by a magician for another person, it should be followed by a spiritual cleansing and a blessing.

REVERSING A SPELL WITH EARTH

The following spell is especially effective against those spells which have been placed with earth. It should be used against curses which have been cast to prevent you from growing economically or prevent you from stabilizing your income. This spell comes from the Pennsylvania Hex practice, and the Hexenmeister who gave it to me swears by it.

Take a small white cup (like the teacups used in Chinese restaurants) and fill it about half full with earth or potting soil. Place the cup in the corner of your bedroom and pray over it as follows:

> Thou art earth of which this whole world is made. Be thou my earth, and take unto thyself all that is sent against me. Bear thou that which is sent against me as Jesus Christ bore the sins of the whole world.

Leave the dirt in the corner of your bedroom for a week, and then cast it out the back door of your house. If you don't have a back door, use the front door. Wait one night and then wash the cup with cold water. You may refill the cup with dirt and repeat the spell if you wish.

You can place the cup in any corner you wish – the corner nearest the bed, for example.

REVERSING A SPELL WITH AIR

This method of reversing a spell is particularly effective against spells which have been placed through the air element. The air element includes gossip, slander and all forms of spoken spells. This spell has been used to halt slanderous testimony in a lawsuit. You may use this spell for yourself, or for someone else. It frees you from slander. When done on a windy day, this spell has particularly strong effect in returning the spell to the one who cast it.

Take about a teaspoon of finely ground sugar, add about a quarter teaspoon of white flour and a pinch of finely ground salt. Mix these in the palm of your hand while concentrating on your desire to be free of curses. Blow the powder out of an open window and immediately say:

Here I stand in innocence; protect me oh Lord!

REVERSING A SPELL WITH IRON

In certain cases spells are cast using iron. These spells are particularly malignant, for they often involve the use of iron to cause accidents to the person who has been cursed. A person who is under the influence of this type of spell may suddenly begin to have accidents with knives, have progressively worse automobile accidents, and generally run afoul of sharp objects, machinery and so forth.

Place three iron rings (the kind used for key rings) in an 8 ounce glass full of drinking water. Then cover the water glass with a clean white handkerchief, and let it stand overnight in the light of the moon.

At sunrise the following day the victim of the curse must drink the water, which instantly breaks the curse. The curse usually returns to the one who sent it, but it may also dissipate into the universe.

REVERSING A SPELL WITH
THE LOW JOHN METHOD

This is a favorite method of reversing a spell in the Gulta practice of "root working." It is used extensively among the black population of the southern United States. The root known as "Low John" (or southernwood root, *Carlina acaulis*, or ground thistle) is gathered and dried. If you feel you have become the recipient of a curse or spell, you take a small piece of the root and chew it thoroughly while concentrating on the curse (or spell) and its effects on you. Once the piece of root has been reduced to a pulp, it should be vigorously spat out on the ground.

This will cast the curse back to the sender. To keep it from returning, you should carry a piece of the root in your pocket for seven days. At the end of seven days the piece of root should be vigorously cast on the ground.

3 *Water Spells*

It is said that human beings were created from the spiritual force of water. This physical manifestation of water relates to the spiritual manifestation of the primordial water element. The water element relates to our emotional force or emotional power – the most powerful force we have.

One of the distinguishing characteristics of the human being is a strong emotional nature, and the desire to search for stimulation of this emotional nature. The drive for emotional fulfillment has always been a prime motivating force.

Because of the connection between our emotional natures and the water element, it is no wonder that water is one of the most common instruments for the transmission of magical effects. It acts directly on our emotional natures. The religious use of water – by Roman Catholics with their holy water, or the Jewish mikveh purification baths – is well known. However, the magical uses of water are not so well known, and in many cases they have been misunderstood to a remarkable degree.

The great Austrian scholar Franz Bardon mentions that water is able to accumulate more energy when it is very cold.[1] He does not discuss the variations in types of water in any depth, nor does he indicate the physical changes in water that take place during the course of a year, but he does say that water can accommodate more energy at 39°F and less energy when heated to temperatures over 99°F. Seasonal changes relating to water were researched by the alchemists of the Paracelsus Research Society of Salt Lake City, Utah.

It is important to understand what happens in the astral realms as a result of the application of teas, washes, etc., so the first thing to understand in magical practice is how to work with water. Teas and washes are made from it. As you know, water is influenced by two major and obvious variations – it is either fresh or salty. Water from the ocean contains salt and other minerals, and it is not drinkable. Lake water is usually fresh, as are rain water and melted snow. And fresh water is drinkable. Magico-religious traditions understand these two distinctions because salt water was ruled by one deity and fresh water by another. This dates back to ancient Babylonia.

The second thing to consider is the astrological influence present when you draw or prepare water. Water is an excellent accumulator of the force Franz Bardon referred to as "magnetism," and it will accept the magnetism of the magician's prayer, as well as the universal life force of the magician's desire. Water will uncritically accept the magnetism present in the universe when it is prayed over, which means that the astral nature of the time of the prayer is added to the force of the prayer. If the astral force at the time of the prayer conflicts with the prayer itself, limitations will be placed on the effect of the spell. Your prayer will fix a moment in time, so you should be careful when you use water.

In many magical practices a distinction is made between the various sources of the water and their effects. *Spiritual*

---

[1] Franz Bardon, *Initiation into Hermetics* (Albuquerque, NM: Brotherhood of Life, 1981).

Cleansing provides some basic information about this. When you are able to observe that various kinds of water have various "feelings" or vibrations, as they are often called, you are well on the way to understanding some of the principles of magic. You can cover a sufficiently large range of work with ordinary tap water or bottled spring water available from the grocery store. It is usually not necessary to complicate things beyond this, as simple tap water will do as well in most spells as the more difficult to obtain products.

Cold water is preferred in most magical work, as it seems to hold the "charge" of the magician's prayer better than warm water. Generally, but dependent upon the requirements of the specific practice, water is simply prayed over and then used as desired. When you add herbs, oils, colors, or perfumes to water you do so to enhance the ability of the prayer to do the work which is being requested. The water is usually the accumulator of the magical prayer or charge.

ADDING INFLUENCES TO WATER

There are a variety of simple methods for adding specific influences to water. This has been highly developed in the healing arts and a variety of methods are in use. In India, the Ayurvedic healers developed a system of healing which uses water to capture the vital essence of gemstones. Metal pieces are placed in water which is then used for the treatment of specific conditions. Flower petals, placed on the surface of a bowl of water and exposed to sunlight, are the basis for the preparation of the Bach Flower Essences discovered by Dr. Edward Bach in England. The "vital essence," or what is called "akasha," of the material passes into the water, which accumulates it. In the case of the Bach Flower Essences, and in some of the Ayurvedic gemstone healing solutions, the vital essence of the flower or gem is placed into the water by the vital essence of the sun. The water is the passive accumulator of this force.

Solarized water is simply water which has been placed in the sunlight. The vital essence of the sun enters into the water in this way. The astrological aspects or the placement of the sun and moon may also be considered to determine the best time to prepare a particular solarized water. It is sometimes specified that a particular spell be made with "water which has never seen the light of the sun."

Moon water, as the name suggests, is water which has been exposed to the light of the full moon. Again, it may be necessary to inquire into the lunar aspects and other astrological factors to determine just what kind of water is being produced. For example, the sun and moon are joined at the new moon, and it is difficult – if not impossible – to prepare "new moon water" which is not also "solarized water."

From the above it is easy to see that it is quite possible to practice a full range of magical operations using only water as the medium for the magical charge. Some magicians have large collections of every conceivable type of magical water. This becomes a bulky process however, as the average person doesn't have the storage space for such an extensive collection of waters. And you don't really need them.

SOLARIZED HEALING WATERS

Healing water may be prepared by placing tap water into a clean bottle, exposing it to sunlight, and then praying over it for the healing of a specific person or condition. The same water may be prepared over the course of a year by filling a green bottle with tap water and exposing the bottle to sunlight on the day after the new moon. If this is done with the new moon in each of the astrological signs over the course of a year, a complete set of twelve healing waters will be obtained. You can use this water for healing by placing a few drops of the healing water in a small glass with a teaspoonful of tap water. Pray over the glass for relief of the condition with which the individual is afflicted. The dose should be repeated four or five times a day until remission occurs. As with any natural healing method, healing with water is a very slow process, so it is best to consult a physician and place yourself under his or her treatment, using this method as an adjutant rather than as a primary form of healing.

In order to solarize healing water, remember that the unique healing property comes from the color of the glass bottle and the vital energy of the sun. To induce energy in a lethargic person, the water should be placed in a red bottle, while a blue bottle will provide a calming effect. Using a yellow glass bottle will stimulate the mind, shaking off mental dullness. Colored glass bottles which will pass the rays of the sun are difficult to obtain, so green wine bottles are usually used for solarization.

If you want to make a more penetrative or active version of the healing waters, use bottled spring water instead of tap water. Spring water is considered to be somewhat more active in nature, but there is little difference between it and tap water. If you live in a place where your water comes from underground sources, you will find your tap water as satisfactory as most spring water.

There is no standard procedure for exposing water to sunlight. Place the bottle on a windowsill. The water will accumulate the most energy when it is exposed to the light of the sun between sunrise and noon on the day following the new moon. Once the water is prepared, store it in a dark place, or at least keep it out of the light of the sun.

To use the twelve solarized waters effectively, you must treat the body with water solarized in the sign of the zodiac that rules the part of the body you wish to heal. This will send the energy of the new moon in that sign to the part of the body affected. See Table 1 on page 22 for a complete list. Healing is assisted by the energy of the moon and the prayer you say over the water. For example, let's say that you want to preserve the appearance of your skin. According to astrological theory, the skin itself is ruled by Capricorn, while its beauty is ruled by Libra. If you were to use solarized water for this treatment you would add a few drops of Libra water to a teaspoon of tap water and rub it on your skin. You might also wish to add a few drops of the healing water to your regular bath. Needless to say, like any other holistic or natural healing method, you cannot use this system of therapy on anyone other than yourself.

You cannot set yourself as a "water healer" without a degree to practice medicine.

You will discover there are times when solarized water is not of a healing nature. For example, you should not make solarized water during a solar eclipse. These "spoiled" waters should either be discarded or used for work which is more attuned to their nature. You can solarize perfectly acceptable water on the second day following the new moon if the water made on the first day does not meet the healing quality necessary.

Preparing a set of solarized waters can be an interesting exercise. At best it will teach you to notice the changes of the seasons and the way the quality of the water changes in accordance with the vibrations or influences of the astral universe at the time. If the exercise is approached as an exercise in self-discipline and development, it will pay dividends which

Table 1. Parts of the Body Ruled by Moon Sign*

Sign	Part of Body Ruled
Aries	Head, Face, Brain
Taurus	Neck, Throat, Cerebellum, Ears
Gemini	Arms, Hands, Shoulders, Lungs, Blood
Cancer	Breast, Stomach, Chest, Digestive Organs
Leo	Heart, Back, Spine
Virgo	Bowels, Intestine, Abdomen
Libra	Skin, Kidneys
Scorpio	Urino-Genital System, Nose, Bladder, Appendix
Sagittarius	Hips, Thighs, Arteries
Capricorn	Knees, Bones, Joints, Teeth
Aquarius	Legs, Ankles, Blood Circulation
Pisces	Feet and Toes

*This information was extracted from: *A Beginners Guide to Practical Astrology* by Vivan E. Robson. Published by Samuel Weiser, York Beach, Maine, 1976, pp. 71–73.

will be of more value than any possible medical use, for it will assist you to attune yourself with the world around you.

Having looked at water in its relatively pure state, we shall now look at its more complicated uses. For the most part this relates to making *teas* from herbs, but you can also add other things to enhance the qualities of water. There is no real difference between the water of an herb and an herbal tea used in herbal medicine. Magical teas are frequently diluted or colored with food color to make a specific water. In some cases perfumes are added for various purposes. Magic waters that are sold in magic stores often have many other ingredients added to them. In most cases, additions are made to increase sales appeal. You NEVER use magical water or tea internally.

MAKING WATER FOR MAGICAL USE

There is one rule you must commit to memory if you wish to make any kind of water into a herbal tea. It applies to healing as well as to magic with herbs, and is one of the few rules which applies to both arts. The rule is that leaves and flowers must be steeped, while roots and barks should be boiled. Until you have at least several years experience working with herbs there are no exceptions to this rule. There are a few exceptions which relate to specific advanced spells. Meanwhile, do not experiment!

Most of the herbs used in magical work are not the same as those you use for healing. Not only are different parts of the herb used, but some magical herbs have no place in the wildest and most eclectic herbal pharmacopoeia. The universal life force of the herb is extracted when you use herbs for healing or for magic, but that is the only similarity. If you use herbs for healing as well as for magic it might be noted that when your healing herbs lose their "virtue" from age or poor storage they may still be strong enough to use magically. The opposite condition does not hold true at all. Some magical herbs are simply members of a general family of herbs, and any member of that family will do. Others must be taken from very specific plants, under very specific conditions to obtain the virtue desired. Again – NEVER DRINK magical herbal teas. They are not meant for internal use!

There are two general methods for preparing magical herbal teas. They give different effects, depending on the prayer made over them at the time they are "brought to life." The two methods depend upon the temperature of the water used in making the teas. The cold method, using room temperature or cooler water, is preferred for fresh picked herbs and flowers. The cold method allows the water to absorb the astral magnetic influence of the herb as well as some of the "akashic" influence – the influence of the universal life force of the herb. In the hot method you use some form of boiling water, and only the akashic influence or its universal life force content transfers to the water. Any magnetic influence in the herb tea must be added by the prayer of the magician when the herb is used.

It is quite possible to have clients make teas by the cold method for their own use. However, teas made by the hot process should be prepared by the magician. Or the magician could give a few ounces of water (which the magician has prayed over) to the client to be added to the hot tea once it has reached room temperature. Another way of dealing with this is to purchase small (single service) bottles of vodka, which the magician prays over, and these could be added by the client to the completed herbal tea. In this way herbal baths, cleansers, or other herbally based spells used by far-away clients will be as effective as the ones actually made by the magician. Vodka will take a good magical charge, especially if it is a higher proof. Vodka also has the ability of preserving herbal teas that are not refrigerated.

The Cold Herbal Tea Method

In order to make a cold herbal tea you need a clean jar with a fairly wide mouth, such as a mason jar. Fill the jar with the fresh herbs or flowers, but don't pack them down tightly. Once the jar is filled with herbs, add sufficient tap or spring water to fill the jar within an inch or so of its top. All the herbs should be under the water. Place the filled bottle in the refrigerator or some other cool place for a week. If the mixture was made for use as a sprinkle it is now ready. If you want to store the herb tea, you can either strain out the herbs or leave them in. You should add a few ounces of vodka in any event, as it assists in retarding spoilage.

If you have made the herbal mixture by the cold process for a bath, you should use the bath as soon as possible after the tea is ready, but do not add vodka. Alcohol of any kind has an effect of its own in a bath, and is best kept away from any bath you might take. Using any alcoholic beverage in a bath will encourage many people to drink alcohol.

The Hot Herbal Tea Method

Bring about ten or twelve ounces of water to a boil in an iron or stainless steel pot. A ceramic pot can be used, but aluminum pots should be avoided. Add the pieces of root bark or seeds, and allow the mixture to simmer for ten to fifteen minutes at a low boil. Remove from the heat and allow the mixture to cool to room temperature. You can strain out the pieces of root bark or seeds by passing the liquid through cheesecloth or a tea strainer. If the liquid is going to be stored for any length of time, two or three ounces of vodka should be added to retard spoilage.

To make a tea of flowers or dried herbs you would bring the ten or twelve ounces of water to boil in the same way. Use an iron, stainless steel, or ceramic pot to boil the water, as you did for the root and bark. When you use flowers or dried leaves, you pour the boiling water over about a teaspoon of the dried or ground herb in a bowl. Allow the mixture to stand and steep until it reaches room temperature. The solids may be strained out with cheesecloth or a tea strainer, and the finished tea can be bottled for storage if desired. Add about two ounces of vodka to each eight ounces (or cup) of the finished herbal tea.

In most cases it is advisable to make up only as much of the tea as you will need within the next few months. Most of these preparations do not store well, even with the addition of vodka (or other alcohol) as a preservative. When you open a bottle of herbal tea and are assailed by an odor of decay it is best to close it up again and discard the entire mixture, bottle and all. It may not seem obvious, but the essential quality of a product will usually pass to its most negative form through the action of bacteria. In short, this means that if the tea has spoiled, don't use it, for you may make a harmful situation rather than a cure.

The reason for using iron or ceramic pots is not obvious until you recall that aluminum is not a natural metal. Iron and stainless steel occur in nature. Passing energy through them in the form of heat transmits the virtue of Mars, the planetary ruler of iron, to the material being boiled or to the water being heated. Ceramics are also naturally occurring materials, and pyrex-type products are the modern cousins of the clay pots made by our ancestors. Heat energy is not distorted when it passes through these materials.

Treat herbs with respect and they will give you the same consideration. You are working with their non-physical properties when you work with herbs magically. Your ability to work with them at all is a gauge of your ability to feel their essence at work, for you recognize that they are a part of the same divine creation which you inhabit.

WAR WATER

War Water (or iron water) was used to treat anemia by folk healers many years ago. It is not a particularly effective method for treating anemia, and there are far better ways to correct iron deficiencies today. It is almost never used medically by folk healers any more, but it has retained its value in magical practice.

Magically, iron water is used to gain protection or to launch magical attacks. It is called War Water because it is one of the most useful weapons for engaging in psychic warfare. It has this reputation because of the superiority of iron weapons over the older weapons of bronze and stone. Iron is the metal of the planet Mars, the planet astrologers credit with ruling warfare and combat, as well as sex. Used for either defense or attack, war water is a strong carrier of the negative emotional energy used in magical battles.

Iron is found in many urban water supplies. Naturally occurring iron water is not really any better than the homemade product. In some cases the homemade product is far superior, as natural iron water may also include undesirable ingredients. The following formula for War Water will produce a material that has a very strong and workable quality to it.

Place about 3/4 pound of cut iron nails into a large (2 quart) bottle. "Cut nails" are the old fashioned nails that have a rectangular cross-section. They are still available from hardware stores as they are used as masonary nails. We use cut nails because they have a rough finish, and will rust easily. Add a half pint of drinkable tap water. Allow this to stand for eight or ten days until the nails begin to rust. Once the rusting process begins, add a quart of tap water. You can store the bottle in the refrigerator, or leave it in a cool place in your home. The bottle must be opened occasionally to allow enough air to enter to continue the rusting process.

Once the water has a definite tinge of rust, usually about a week to ten days after you have added the quart of water, it is ready to use. Should you find any trace of mould or bacteria on the water, you should discard the water, the bottle and the nails. I have never had this happen, but I have heard that it can.

To use the water, remove about two ounces of the rusty water from the bottle at a time. Add fresh tap water as water is removed and you will have an almost continuous supply of the water. As this water is not often used, even in the midst of a psychic war, it is not necessary to concern yourself about running out once you have made some. A little war water goes a long way.

Using War (or Iron) Water

There are a number of ways that you can use iron water. It is generally used for protection, and you can take a bath to protect yourself, or you can use it in your home to protect yourself against specific spells. This water is especially beneficial when you want to protect yourself against acts of violence of any sort.

Protection Bath: Take two ounces of War Water and add it to a tub of water. Pray over the tub for general protection in life, as well as for protection against the specific influence you wish to have removed from your life. This could be as specific as "The thoughts of N.N.," "The evil work of N.N.," or so forth. You could also pray for general protection, but this should be done only rarely. Once a year is sufficient for a general protection bath, and it should be taken after you have protected your home with the war water as given below. Soak in the tub for at least eight minutes, immersing yourself completely at least four times. You should air dry after this bath to maintain the protection around you. It is best if you avoid taking any other bath, even for cleansing, for twenty-four hours.

This bath should not be taken more often than once a week. Usually, taken twice a year, this bath will protect you from the effects of any magician of better than average ability.

Protection Against Specific Spells: To protect your home or apartment against the type of spell that is cast by placing something in the doorway or on the steps of a house, add two ounces of War Water to a mop bucket of water. Pray over the water to remove all negative influences from your doorway, your steps, and whatever else you intend to mop. Then mop the surfaces, wringing out the mop into another bucket. When you have finished, pour the mop water and the wringings into a street or a roadway.

If you are going to declare psychic war on someone you should mop your stairs, porch, doorway, and any outside surfaces of your home on which anything can be cast or thrown before you begin the war. This ensures that you will be protected when the other person's inevitable counterattack comes. In most cases War Water will cause any spell which is placed on your doorstep to rebound instantly to the sender.

Protection of a Home: This spell is especially suited to protecting a home from acts of violence, whether the violence is psychic or physical. This spell may be done annually if desired. The best day to do this in a Christian home is on the feast day of St. John the Baptist, on June 24th. In a pagan or non-religious home, the best day is the day of the summer solstice, about the 21st of June.

Add two ounces of War Water to a mop bucket of water. Pray over the water for the protection you want. If you are a Christian, you should pray in the name of St. John the Baptist. Lightly mop the house out, from top to bottom, front to back. Wring your mop into another bucket. Throw out the water and the wringings from the back door of the house if you have a back door. Rinse out the bucket and mop and pour the rinse water down the toilet. If you don't have a back door, flush the water down the toilet and rinse out the bucket and mop and flush that water, too.

TAR WATER

Creosote was once a common household cleanser. It is no longer available, however, as many people feel that creosote causes cancer. Tar Water has been used in the past for the same kinds of cleansing as creosote was used for. It is almost as effective as creosote, and much easier to obtain. To make Tar Water you will need access to a wood burning fireplace. Tar Water is occasionally made using roofing tar. This is not the same product, for roofing tar has a mineral origin – it is made from petroleum. Roofing tar and coal tar are not the same as wood tar, and cannot be used for the removal of thoughtforms.

To make Tar Water you will need about a quart of wood tar, the sticky stuff that comes from the chimney of wood-burning fireplaces. Place the tar in a large bucket. You should use a bucket you are not particularly attached to, as you will find that it is not going to be very good for cleaning any more. Mix about a gallon of water with the tar, stirring briskly with a wooden stick for ten or fifteen minutes. Allow the tar to settle for two or three hours, and pour the water off into a clean container. Let the water settle again and once again pour it off, filtering it through cheesecloth into smaller bottles you can close.

Tar Water usually does not go bad, so it is not necessary to add vodka to it as a preservative. It will settle out further in time, forming a dark oily ring around the bottle. It is necessary that the bottle be shaken vigorously before any water is taken from it. Another approach is to add a small amount of dish-washing soap – a few drops per quart of tar water. This will dissolve the oil in the tar water so it does not stain the bottle.

Using Tar Water

Tar Water, like creosote, is used to remove heavy thought-forms from a person, place, or thing. It is used to remove the kind of heavy and obsessive thoughts that come from the deep emotions of grief, pain, and loss. It can also be used as a floorwash or mopping compound to remove heavy negative emotions left by quarrels, fights, or arguments.

If you recently moved into new living quarters and find yourself quarreling more often with those with whom you live, you may be being influenced by the thoughtforms of the previous residents. Negative thoughtforms can remain in the same location for many years, influencing everyone who comes in contact with them. Using Tar Water floorwash throughout the living space will destroy these thoughtforms, or at least weaken them enough to reduce their effect on your family.

Tar Water Bath: For a tub bath, use a cup of tar water to a tub full of bath water. Pray over the bath for the release of the thoughtforms, or for cleansing and protection. The person being cleansed should soak in the tub for about ten minutes, trying to let go of all inner turbulence.

Tar Water Floorwash: For a floorwash, use about a cup of tar water in a bucket of water. Clean the floors first, and then use the floorwash as a final coating. In some cases it may seem as if the room has been redecorated; it can become much brighter once the old thoughtforms have been cleaned out.

INDIGO WATER

Indigo is made from a plant. It used to be one of the principal ingredients in blue dyes and in laundry blueing. As it was a fairly rare and expensive commodity it quickly gained a magical reputation. Pieces of indigo were carried as good luck charms, and indigo began to be used for all sorts of things.

Indigo does have certain useful properties, and it was the discovery of these properties which gave the material its initial reputation. As a dye, and as a color, indigo has the ability to strengthen the astral nature of anything to which it is applied. Natural indigo (or the color indigo from natural sources) will act faster in this respect than an aniline dye of the same color. This is because of the greater harmony of the natural dye with the natural flow of the universal life force.

The astral world is fed by those things which affect the human senses. Thus, color, scent, flavor, and texture are, or may be regarded, as foods to the astral realm. This is one of the reasons why physical offerings are made to the forces of the universe, and these forces are known as gods to their worshippers.

Indigo water is made from ordinary household blueing, either dissolved or diluted with tap water. The powdered blueing will settle on standing, so the bottle must be shaken before each use. If it is impossible to find blueing, which is fast going out of style in this age of wash-and-wear, blue food coloring may be used. An intense blue color is what is required in the bottle of Indigo Blue Water.

Using Indigo Blue Water

Indigo Blue Water is used to strengthen and add power to charms of all sorts. A few drops of the water are placed on the charm and spread over it before the charm is prayed over. The water is allowed to evaporate from the charm, or to be absorbed by it. This treatment will strengthen the astral field of the charm, and allow it to accept a greater charge of emotional energy from the magician when it is charged by prayer.

Indigo Blue Water Baths: Indigo Blue Water is very useful in baths for it strengthens the aura and, thus, the astral body. When it is used for this purpose it is used in a soaking bath. The individual taking the bath should relax in the tub for about twenty minutes. About one to three tablespoons of Indigo Blue Water is added to the tub for this bath. For the best effect, the person taking the bath should submerge completely in the bath several times.

Other Uses for Indigo Blue Water: Indigo Blue Water is frequently used in conjunction with sea water to balance the energy flow. To balance your energy, it is applied to your spinal column following a thorough spiritual cleansing.

A mixture of Indigo Water and sea water is frequently found on the altar of practitioners of a number of magico-religious practices. Those who keep this symbol do so as an obligation or a duty, it is not done as a casual act. The fact that you see someone do it does not mean that you should follow their example.

FLOWER AND FRUIT WATERS

Flower and fruit waters may be made from flower petals and fruit peelings by the cold method. The flowers or fruit are placed in water and left in the refrigerator for a week or so. If you wish to keep these waters you should add vodka to retard spoilage. Water will accept the vibrations of most flowers and fruits, but not much of the scent will pass into the water. Usually there is enough of the quality present to allow the water to be used magically, but there is insufficient scent to allow its use as perfume. Once the flower petals or fruit peelings have served their purpose in making the water they should be strained out and discarded.

There are three favorite waters in Indian and Middle Eastern cooking which may be used directly as flower waters. They have a better quality than the homemade product, and are usually more effective when they are used as sprays. These are rose water, orange water, and orris water. In some cases lemon and lime waters can also be purchased, but these are considerably more difficult to locate.

Once you can identify the effects of fruit and flower essences you can make up your own. These essences make a useful spray in the home, sprayed from an ordinary "spritzer" spray bottle. Until you can identify the effects of a spray by the vibration, you are better off using only the sprays mentioned here.

Rose Water: Will act to purify any place where it is sprayed or used as a floorwash. It will act to remove some thoughtforms or heavy vibrations. It can make a home a lighter place to live in. It is not a cure-all, however, and will neither remove heavy thoughtforms nor break curses.

Orange Water: This water smells a bit like orange blossoms – the traditional wedding flower. It acts to encourage the display of emotions – which is useful if the emotions displayed are positive! It is good to use if you are expecting company for a dinner or a party.

Orris Water: Used to promote communication between people. It is best sprayed into the air before a gathering takes place. Its effect as a floorwash is not very lasting. It seems to act to encourage people to speak their minds on any subject, and can be useful for preparing conference rooms and meeting halls.

Lemon Water: Brings a refreshing and stimulating feeling to the place where it is sprayed. It can also suppress those who talk too much.

Lime Water: Lime water calms places where an excess of energy is present. It is useful in a children's playroom as a spray or a floorwash. It has only a temporary effect, but it can assist you in getting children to bed on time if you spray the room while they are having dinner. There is a commercial lime water which is available which is not made from the lime, and it will not have the same effect. Be sure you make your own water from the fruit of the lime.

For parties and social occasions a spray made from rose and orris water will make the occasion a bit more festive. It lightens the vibrations and makes people a bit more communicative. There are further suggestions for sprays in the section on herbs. They are all made from herbal teas. We will now look at the predecessors of sprays – the herbal sprinkles.

WATER SPRINKLES

Sprinkles and sprays serve a similar purpose. They change the feeling of a place. They are usually made from a herb tea with a bit of vodka added to retard spoilage. In most cases the herb tea is one which is made by the cold process in the refrigerator. The sprinkle is placed in the room by sprinkling from a bowl by hand, while the spray is placed in the room using a spritzer sprayer.

Many occult and curio shops sell aerosol pressurized sprays. The water based sprinkles and sprays made from herbs and spices are much less expensive. The homemade product actually works better, as the store items are usually made of perfume and do not have much of the herb or spices in them. One of the nice things about sprinkles and sprays is that the effects are not as long lasting as those found with incenses or other work. Thus it becomes possible to change the effects in a room several times during the course of a day.

To make up a sprinkle, use the herb tea directly from the bottle in the refrigerator. Pour about two ounces in a bowl and sprinkle it around the room freely. Be sure to get some into the corners of the room, but unless you like to wash walls, try to avoid flicking the sprinkle onto the walls as it will waterspot.

In the section on herbs there are a number of herbs mentioned as sprinkles, along with the purpose for their use. As with everything else used with magical intent, it is important to pray over the sprinkle for the effect you desire before you begin flicking it around the room.

MAKING BATHS

In the section on herbs several herbs are mentioned that can be used as a bath. These baths are made by using an herb tea. About eight ounces of the tea are required for a tub bath.

In the case of a blended tea, made from two or more herbs, it is better to make the teas separately and then blend the strained teas together. In certain cases this is not done, the two herbs being mixed together and only one tea made. It is important to read the instructions in each case. For the most part it is probably better to stick with the baths listed as examples in this section or the single herb baths in the section on herbs. Experimenting will often cause more trouble than it is worth.

All these baths are intended to work on the spiritual body, so they should be taken as soaking baths. This also means that a physical bath should usually precede the spiritual bath – no soap or bath oil should be used in a herbal bath. As the bath intends to work on the spiritual body, it is better to air dry after an herbal bath.

In taking an herbal bath, the entire body should be exposed to the herb. This requires that the person soak in the tub for six to eight minutes, immersing the whole body completely several times. This procedure will allow the herbal bath to have its best effect on you.

Using herbal baths occasionally is an excellent way of keeping yourself on top of the world around you. It is not a cure-all, but it is an improvement over the usual state of spiritual neglect which most people practice. A few of the cleansing and protective baths may convince you to make them a regular part of your life.

A Bath for Protection Against Negativity

This bath will release negative influences and maintain you in a protected state for ten to twelve hours. It is a good bath to take if you have to visit negative or hostile people. The bath provides a sort of "armor" that protects you throughout the course of your visit. Place in a two quart bowl:

7 fresh garlic cloves
1 pinch dried thyme
1/4 teaspoon dried basil
1 pinch dried sage

Pour a quart of boiling water over the mixture and allow the water to cool while the mixture steeps. Strain out the spices and pour the mixture into a tub full of bath water. Bathe in the tub for seven minutes, praying for the release of negativity and protection from negativity. Immerse your body at least three times. In this bath it is the interaction of the herbal mixture that permeates the bath, giving it its special character.

A Bath for Increased Business

If you work for yourself, or if your income depends on tips, you can increase your earnings by taking this bath. It is designed specifically to provide a temporary increase in the money supply. It should be taken shortly after a new moon for the longest lasting results. However, it should not be taken more frequently than once every three or four months. Too frequent use nullifies its effects. Place in a two quart bowl:

7 teaspoons dried parsley
1 teaspoon ground cinnamon
1 teaspoon ground nutmeg
1 teaspoon brown sugar

Pour one quart of boiling water over the mixture and allow it to cool to room temperature. Then strain the liquid into a half tub of bath water. Bathe for seven minutes and pray for an increase in finances while you are in the tub. Do not wonder or speculate as to where the money will come from; just know that you will receive it.

The Bridal Bath Spell

The purpose of this bath is to remove sexual fears and blocks from a woman who is about to be married. It may also be used under other circumstances, but my source specified that the bath is for women and is to be taken three days before the wedding. A friend who used it said that it made her more freely orgasmic. It certainly can't hurt in any case.

Combine 3 heaping teaspoons of dried oregano, and 1 heaping teaspoon of dried basil. Place in a bowl and pour a quart of boiling water over the mixed herbs. When the mixture cools to room temperature strain out the herbs and add the tea to a tub of bath water. You should remain in the tub for at least eight minutes and immerse yourself a total of eight times. Air drying is very much preferred in a bath of this kind, and you should not take another bath for at least twenty-four hours.

A Bath to Release Emotional Energy

Unresolved conflicts are very damaging in daily life. As these emotional conflicts and stresses are usually deeply buried within, you do not usually examine them consciously. The trick in dealing with conflict is to release rather than to hold on to it. Unfortunately, this usually requires that you deal with conflicts using your rational mentality, something which few people are equipped to do. The following bath will assist in the release of conflicts and associated emotional energy, whether or not the conflict has presented itself to your conscious mind.

Draw a tub of bath water and add 1 cup of sifted rye flour to it, stirring the flour in well. You should soak in the tub for about twenty minutes, immersing yourself at least four or five times. You should consciously relax in the tub, releasing any tension which you might feel.

A General Astral Cleansing Bath

Psychiatrists who follow the philosophy of Dr. Wilhelm Reich often prescribe this bath for their patients. They use it to release astral dirt and thoughtforms, also known as DOR. A friend of mine claims this bath rebalances the electromagnetic field of the person taking it. It has a strong effect on many people, and it should be taken only when you are able to go to sleep afterwards.

I have recommended this bath successfully for those who suffer from over-excitable natures. It gives them at least some degree of calm. I usually accompany this bath with a recommendation to see a professional therapist.

Draw a tub of cool water and add 1 pound of bicarbonate of soda and 1 pound of sea salt. Mix the water thoroughly to be certain that the salts are dissolved. Enter the tub and immediately immerse yourself. Remain in the tub for at least twenty minutes, immersing yourself frequently and relaxing between immersions. When you leave the tub you should dry thoroughly and go to bed and sleep until you awaken.

If you are greatly disturbed after this bath you should consult a professional therapist, as it means you need to discuss your problems with someone.

A Skin Tonic Bath for Negativity

This bath may be taken either to release negative influences or to assist you in toning your skin. The bath has been used as a cosmetic aid for many years, but because it also has some benefit in releasing negative influences it is included here. This bath can be used as a regular bath—with soap, bath oil, and whatever. The usual time you spend in the tub is usually sufficient for this bath for the bath will allow the release of minor negative influences while you bathe. Add the following to a tub of bath water:

1 cup apple cider vinegar
1 teaspoon salt

If you wish to use this bath strictly to release negativity, bathe for five minutes with a minimum of three full immersions. Pray for the release of any negative energy around you.

A Bath for Self-Discipline

When you have difficulty in dealing with the everyday situations of life, you are probably experiencing two very similar problems. First, you may have a problem with self esteem, and second, you probably lack self-discipline. These two difficulties seem to feed on each other, and the end result is that your life becomes a tangled mess.

The usual solution to these difficulties is to seek some form of therapy. Taking this bath in the initial stages of therapy will usually assist you to gather enough self-discipline to see at least part of your problem dissipate to the extent that you can deal with what remains.

The bath has an action which firms up willpower and it will temporarily remove anything which is acting as an impediment to your will. You need some form of therapy to overcome learned difficulties, and this bath is not a substitute for psychotherapy or any other form of therapy. It is merely an assistance in the early stages of your attempt to break out of a negative life. It is at best an aid, not a remedy.

The bath is also useful if you wish to break a habit pattern with which you have become consciously identified. An example is giving up the habit of smoking. The bath will give some assistance by strengthening your willpower to overcome the addiction to tobacco. Here again, the bath is an aid, not a remedy.

The difficulty with relying on magical aids to drive off negative influences or change character is that there is always something within that calls the negative influence to you in the first place. This "something" is not removed by the bath. It must be removed through the exertion of personal effort. If you cannot make the effort, or will not make the effort to remove the "something," the difficulty will return. Any magical spell, charm, bath, or whatever can only allow your astral nature to see just what it would be like if this "something" were to be permanently gone. It is then up to your astral, mental, and animal nature to get rid of it.

If you have tried to work with people over any length of time, you are probably aware that most people do not wish to change, they wish to become comfortable. Thus they are not likely to wish to divest themselves of any ingrained habit or negativity. What they want is to learn how to be comfortable with the ingrained habit or negativity that they have.

With these caveats in mind, the Cherry Blossom Bath for self-discipline is still a very useful bath. If for no other reason, you might wish to take one to assist yourself in working some of the other spells in the book!

To make this bath, take a handful of fresh cherry blossoms and place them in a two quart bowl. Pour a quart of boiling water over them and let them steep until the water cools to room temperature. Strain the blossoms out and pour the liquid into a tub of bath water. Soak in the tub for twenty minutes to a half hour, immersing yourself four or five times. Air dry after this bath to keep the vibration or feeling around you as long as possible.

A Bath for Ending Relationships

When relationships between people are ended, either through mutual agreement or divorce, there is still an astral connection between them. The astral connection is caused by their sexual contact, which energizes this connection. This astral connection may cause a great deal of discomfort until it finally weakens over time. There is a simple way to end this astral connection once and for all. This is through the use of a ritual bath made with walnuts. The bath makes it easier for both parties to end the relationship. Don't use this ritual bath if you are not sure if you really want to break the tie.

Simmer six unshelled walnuts in an iron pot full of water. The walnuts should simmer about three hours, with water being added as required. Allow the last quart or so of water to cool to room temperature, remove the walnuts and add the tea to a tub of bath water. When in the tub you should make a sincere prayer to end the relationship. On no account should sexual relations with the other party be resumed after taking the bath.

A Bath for Spiritual Growth

Spiritual power is associated with spiritual growth. If you desire spiritual power you need to look more to spiritual growth as a way to gain that which you seek. There is no external road to true spiritual growth, as the process of growth must be undertaken yourself and you will probably need the guidance of a spiritual teacher.

The following bath can assist in cleaning away the detritus which keeps one from true spiritual growth. It also has the side benefit of making it somewhat easier for the teacher to draw you near. A student who is ready is never too far away from a teacher; you may only be ignorant that the teacher exists.

Take 1 tablespoon of ground white eggshells and 1 tablespoon of ground lotus root powder.

Stir into the bath by hand, and pray over the bath before you enter it. Once in the tub, immerse yourself immediately. Continue to immerse until you have made a total of eight immersions. Then leave the tub and air dry. Do not take another bath for twenty-four hours.

A Mate Tea Bath

Mate tea, made from *Ilex paraguaniensis* leaves, is a very common tea in South America. In addition to its use as a beverage, it is also used as a cleansing bath in spiritual practices from Mexico to Brazil. It is a favorite in many of the Spanish spiritual practices as it has a positive cleansing effect. As a bath it will remove most of the astral detritus of everyday life, and is effective in removing the effects of malochia, as well as breaking minor curses.

Mate tea is available in teabags from health food stores. Use 2 cups of strong mate tea and stay in the tub for six to eight minutes. Immerse yourself at least three times while in the tub. This tea can also be used as a sponge bath. Sponge the solution over yourself after taking a shower or otherwise washing yourself. Air dry after sponging.

A Broom Herb Bath

Broom herb (*Cytisus scoparius*) is used in baths as an astral "broom," clearing out the influences of the lower astral realms. The tops of the broom plant are placed in a pot and about two cups of boiling water are poured over them. Once the mixture has reached room temperature the broom herb is strained out and the liquid added to a tub of bath water.

In this bath, water should be continuously poured over your head while you sit in the tub full of water. After six or eight bowls of water are poured over your head, you should leave the bath and towel dry your hair. Air drying completes the bathing process.

Broom herb tops, like many other herbs, can also be used to make an alcohol. The procedure is to simply soak the herb in ethyl rubbing alcohol for a week or so. The alcohol can be used for cleansing the aura by wiping the body down, or by placing about 3 ounces of the alcohol in the bathtub, and taking a bath as above.

A Clove Bath for Protection

Ground Cloves (*Eugenia aromatica*) may be used as a protection bath. They act to protect you from any negative influences sent either consciously or sub-consciously by others. Before you attend a meeting or interact with people with whom you are likely to have verbal or psychic conflict, a clove bath is recommended.

Pour 2 cups of boiling water over $\frac{1}{2}$ teaspoon of ground cloves. Allow the mixture to steep until it reaches room temperature, and add it to a tub of bath water. Stay in the tub seven or eight minutes, immerse seven times. Pray for protection from all negative influences. Air dry yourself to maintain the protective influence of the bath.

4 *Incense Spells*

The magical influences of water operate most effectively on the astral-emotional nature. We will find that incense also has its special effect. Incense has its greatest effect on the mental-intellectual nature. When we burn incense we are activating the mental plane and manifesting the force of the air elementals. The activation of the mental-intellectual nature by the use of incense also has an effect on the astral-emotional nature as well. When we stimulate the mental-intellectual nature by burning an incense, we stimulate the flow of communication with the forces of the universe. Burning incense also enhances the flow of communication between people. The interested reader may want to read *Incense* and *The Magic of Perfume* for additional information.[1]

---

[1]See Vinci, *Incense* (Wellingborough, England: Thorsons Publishing Group, 1980); and Maple, *The Magic of Perfume* (Thorsons Publishing Group, 1973). Both are now out of print, but worth reading if you can find a copy.

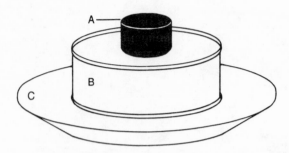

To burn incense without marring furniture, place the charcoal (A) on top of an overturned can (B) placed on a saucer (C).

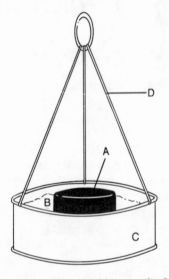

To make a censer, place charcoal (A) on a bed of sand (B) in an empty can (C). Poke three holes in the rim of the can and use wire or chains (D) to suspend the censer.

Figure 1. Two methods of burning incense. Top: using an upside down can with charcoal and incense on top; and bottom: making a censer out of an empty can.

In the more advanced magical techniques used to summon a spirit to visible appearance, incense not only promotes communication with the spirit, but through the medium of the smoke flux it makes it possible for the spirit to manifest to visible appearance with the least possible expenditure of energy. In many of the lesser techniques of magic this dual function of incense plays a large part in gaining the effects desired.

You will find that burning incense is not an elaborate process. The spices and gum resins which are mentioned here are available in many health food, herb, and occult supply stores around the country. Self-lighting charcoals may be purchased at most of these stores, or at religious supply stores in almost every city. Many of the incense mixtures that follow can be made from spices found in your kitchen.

You can make an incense burner from an old catfood or tunafish can and a saucer. Place the can on the saucer and put a self-lighting charcoal on top. Light the edge of the self-lighting charcoal with a match and allow the flame to travel across the surface of the charcoal. This is accomplished with a lot of popping and sparking. Once the charcoal is lit all across its top surface the sparking will stop. You may now add incense to the hot charcoal about a quarter teaspoon at a time. If you wish to do so you can always add more incense to the charcoal after the first batch has gone out.

Once you have experimented with burning incense you may want to try using a censer. A censer is simply an incense burner which is swung by hand. Using a censer will allow you to apply incense throughout your entire living quarters using only one charcoal, for you can carry the incense with you as you apply it throughout your home. You can make a censer from another catfood can and three small pieces of chain. Place some sand in the bottom of the can and a self-lighting charcoal on top. Light the charcoal, and once the sparking has stopped you can put some incense on it. Then pick up the censer by the chain end and swing it gently as you slowly walk through your home. Figure 1 will give you some idea of how this is done. Once you have tried this method you will be surprised how easy it is to do.

When you burn incense in your home you will find that the effects last from four to twelve hours afterward. If you frequently burn similar incenses you will find that the place where they are burned has a tendency to maintain the vibration of the incense blend permanently. If you are comfortable with the incenses you are using this is all right. If the incenses you are using are all calls for help, however, you will find that they become self-defeating. If you burn only incenses which are requests to the universe for help, protection, or money, you will find that their results drop off quickly. The forces of the universe have a tendency to look on this as a case of over-kill, so they will respond to the burning of these incenses less and less and eventually not at all. This is why many of the incenses mentioned in this chapter are marked with a request for infrequent burning. The number of times a year you can safely burn them and still have them work for you is noted.

If you wish to use a number of incenses in your work, or if you wish to burn incense frequently, you should select those which are calming and of a spiritual nature. The area where you will be working will then take on this calming and spiritual vibration. When you have set up the spiritual vibration, other more specific incenses will have the desired effect because the forces of the universe will always respond to a spiritual call. It's only calls based on human greed which are ignored. Specific incenses should only be used for specific tasks, and only when you really need them.

Some people like to burn incense simply to maintain a mystic aura to their living quarters. When this is the only reason for burning incense you should question your motive. I have never met a real magician or occultist who burned incense simply because he or she liked the smell. On the other hand incense is burned by people who would like you to think they are "into" the occult. You must remember that incenses are a powerful tool in magic. Those who misuse powerful tools lose the right to use them constructively.

MIXING AND STORING INCENSE

You will find that the incense formulas presented here will make more incense than you might wish to use at one time.

You can store the surplus in small bottles or plastic jars. Baby food jars are good, so are plastic vitamin tablet bottles. The important point is that they should be kept sealed. Incense, like almost everything else, will deteriorate over time in contact with air. If you keep incense in small sealed containers you will find that it will last almost indefinitely. I have used incense that I have had stored over ten years with good results. In some cases, when certain incenses need to blend together, long term storage enhances the effect. The incenses will not lose their virtue, but they may lose most of their scent if they are left exposed to the air. Spices are said to lose their seasoning qualities after six months in a kitchen. This is not true for their effect as incenses in my experience. You may wish to adopt my own rule of thumb – use the incense unless it looks bad. If it looks bad, throw it away and make up some fresh incense.

I have found that the best way to mix incense is by using a mortar and pestle. I have a good ceramic mortar and pestle given to me by a friend who is a chemist. They may also be found in houseware stores, in a variety of sizes. If you have a mortar which will hold about a cup of liquid you will have one which is the correct size for almost any practical use.

Gum resin incenses, such as frankincense, myrrh and benzoin, are easier to work with and last longer if they are purchased in large lumps and stored in closed containers. This usually makes them difficult to break up and grind in the mortar however. If the pieces to be ground are placed in the refrigerator overnight before they are ground or broken up in the mortar they will be easier to work with. If they are ground to a powder, the excess can be stored in a glass or plastic bottle and used when next required, saving having to grind each batch.

When incenses are made entirely from spices it is often easier to mix them on a piece of paper. The paper may be creased and used as a funnel to place the finished incense in a small bottle, which you can shake to complete the mixing.

Incense is one of our oldest offerings to God, and you should enjoy working with it. Please remember to label and date all the incense you make and keep it out of the reach of children and adults who do not understand its use.

INCENSE FROM THE KITCHEN

Kitchen spices and blends are useful as incenses. The effects they have are indicated on the following list. These simple incenses may become your favorites.

Allspice: Good for social gatherings; increases the flow of conversation and the rapport between people.

Cinnamon: Calming; has a protective vibration. It stimulates the mind to some extent, and it can also bring money into the home. It is good to burn in the nursery, as it has a calming and quieting effect on young children.

Cloves: Psychically protective, it keeps negative thoughtforms out of the place it is burned.

Coffee: Good for protection from negativity; it can put an end to nightmares when it is burned in the bedroom. Better for teenage children than cinnamon.

Mace: Good for self-discipline; aids concentration and strengthens the mental body. It is a spice ruled by Mars and affects the mental plane.

Nutmeg: Makes people feel expansive or jovial. It adds to self-confidence, opens people to being joyous. It is not a sexual incense, but it does promote congeniality.

The following spice blends are used as incenses, about a quarter teaspoon at a time. Their names are indicative of their use.

Blessing of Concord: Cinnamon and allspice combined in equal parts. This places a smooth and witty feeling into the place where it is burned. It encourages social affairs and discourages jealousy between people. A bit of frankincense can be added to raise the vibration.

Mental Ease and Peace: This resulted from a friend's making up an incense from the recipe in the folk song called "Parsley,

Sage, Rosemary and Thyme." Taken in equal parts, it yields an incense which seems to smooth out the vibrations in the place where it is burned. It makes meditation a bit calmer and easier, and calms the home at bedtime. It also seems to relieve mental tension and help those who worry a lot.

Mental Stimulation and Wit: This incense is an example of the positive use of mace – the incense of Mars. It has a mentally stimulating effect and is good for increasing the alertness of those who do mental work. It is not a bad incense for the office or the store, in that it seems to perk things up a bit. It is bad to burn where tempers flare, however. Take two teaspoons of mace and mix with a teaspoon of ground cloves and a teaspoon of ground cinnamon. Burn a quarter teaspoon at a time on a hot charcoal for best results. The remainder can be placed in a small bottle and stored for future use. It improves a bit with a week of ageing.

Blessing Incense: This incense is used to effect a blessing on a person, place, or thing. It is particularly good for blessing a new possession or article of clothing. Pray for what is desired as the incense is burning. Make the incense by mixing a teaspoon of ground bay leaf with a teaspoon of ground cumin. Add a pinch of salt and mix well. Burn a quarter teaspoon at a time on hot charcoal and let the fumes of the incense reach the person or item being blessed.

RITUAL INCENSE

Your most important incense is the ritual incense used to cense an area used for ritual purposes. The following is my own blend, which serves well for most work. Specific rituals call for specific incenses, and in some cases this incense will not do at all. However, you will find that it will serve for most simple ritual work. The incense will not only cleanse an area, but it will also bring in the vibrations required for most work.

Mix the following gum resins either by weight or by volume. A tablespoonful may be crushed in the mortar for use as required. Be sure to label the container and date it so you remember when you prepared it.

> 51% frankincense
> 20% myrrh
> 20% benzoin
> 9% copal[2]

The incense may either be used on the altar or in a censer. It is also useful for fumigations and for censing in spiritual cleansings.

PROTECTIVE INCENSE

This incense is used to protect those occupying the place where it is burned. It was originally devised by Joseph-Antoine Boullan, a well-known occultist of the 19th century. The story of his preparing it for the use of J. K. Huysmans is told in *Eliphas Levi and the French Occult Revival*.[3] The incense was made and blessed in the name of St. John the Baptist.

The incense is made as a stiff gum, formed into small balls or pellets the size of a pea. These can be flattened into wafers if desired. It is to be burned on charcoal with a prayer for protection whenever protection is desired. The incense improves slightly with age as long as it is kept in a closed container which does not allow the camphor gum to evaporate.

Mix in a mortar:

> 1 teaspoon finely ground myrrh powder
> 1 teaspoon frankincense powder
> 1 teaspoon ground cloves
> 1 teaspoon camphor gum (either synthetic from your local drugstore or natural from a store selling Indian foods and spices).

---

[2]You can usually find copal in art supply stores. It is usually used as a paint medium.

[3]Christopher McIntosh, *Eliphas Levi and the French Occult Revival* (York Beach, ME: Samuel Weiser, 1974) p. 190. Now out of print.

If the mixture does not form a gum, add a bit more camphor to bind it. The finished pellets may be rolled or dusted with myrrh powder to make them less sticky if desired.

You use this incense by placing a pellet on a hot charcoal. While the fumes are rising you should pray for the protection you desire. If you are praying from a Christian perspective, you should make your prayer to St. John the Baptist. From a pagan perspective you should address your prayer to the martial or Mars-related deity in the pantheon you use.

To cleanse yourself or another person from negative influences you may use this incense in a fumigation. For information on fumigating yourself or another person see page 55 where fumigation with incense is discussed at length.

HIGH SPIRIT INCENSE

The name "High Spirit Incense" is frequently found on incenses sold in occult or curio shops. It is an incense which attracts higher spiritual forces, and has the effect of protecting, blessing, and generally clearing up the spiritual environment. The incense given below is not what you will find in the occult store, but is actually the incense used by spiritual practitioners. It is made from gum resins, and while it is more costly, it is also much more effective.

If you are only going to work with one or two incenses this is one which you will want to keep on hand. The incense is made in the mortar and sealed in small bottles. You may burn about a quarter teaspoon at a time on charcoal.

> 3 teaspoons frankincense
> 2 teaspoons benzoin gum
> 1 teaspoon myrrh

You may use this incense either in a fixed burner or in a censer. You may also use this incense in a fumigation, especially following a cleansing bath.

MEDITATION INCENSE

This incense is sometimes known as High Church Incense, or Church Incense. The formula we will use contains gum resins, while the occult store product is usually made from perfume oils and wood flour. You will find that our version of the incense has a very spiritual and quiet vibration. It is useful for meditation or for calming a nervous vibration.

This incense is made in the mortar and stored in small closed bottles. You can burn it on charcoal about a quarter teaspoon at a time.

> $2^{1}/_{2}$ teaspoons of frankincense
> 1 teaspoon of myrrh
> 1 teaspoon of copal

You may burn this incense either in a fixed burner or in a censer. You will find that it is best in meditation if you use a fixed burner that remains about six feet away when you are meditating.

INCENSE FOR SWEETENING THE HOME

This incense originated with black Americans in the South. It was a favorite incense in the pre-Civil War South, when resin gums were not available to the black slaves. This incense cheers up the home, settling so called "troubled conditions." It is also good to use around old people, especially those who feel that they have nothing to live for.

Unlike the other incenses made from gums, this incense does not store for more than a week or so. Therefore you should make only the amount you will need for one time.

Mix two or three drops of honey in a quarter teaspoon of brown sugar. Place the resulting paste on a hot charcoal and allow the fumes to fill the house. The odor can be rather strong if it is burned in a room full of people, consequently it is usually better to burn this when you are alone. The vibrations will remain when the rest of the family arrives.

MONEY-DRAWING INCENSE

This incense is useful for opening to door to money. It has gained a very good reputation in money-drawing, as it seems to work when it is used. Having used it myself when in financial need I can testify to its effectiveness. I am sure it will work as well for you, although there are no guarantees in the operation of magic. Burning this incense seems to announce to the universe that more income is needed.

Mix a teaspoon of benzoin gum powder and two teaspoons of cinnamon in a mortar. Burn about a quarter teaspoon at a time on hot charcoal. Cense all the rooms of the house with the incense when you want a lift in your money supply.

This incense must not be over-used, as over-use is a signal that you are unhappy with the divine supply that is being given you. The universe seems to interpret over-use as a sign of greed, and reduces rather than increases the supply. Using this incense three or four times a year is best. You should use it when you are at a low point financially, as this seems to have the best results. It will bring money in to you – don't be impatient. It is important not to wonder where the money will come from, for doing so may act to limit the amount available to you.

CONCENTRATION INCENSE

This incense has been used for many years to encourage concentration when meditating. You may find it valuable when you study. This incense may be burned in your bedroom to aid your mind in directing itself to certain thoughts while you sleep. It is an aid to concentration in general. Mix together well the following spices:

> 3 teaspoons cinnamon
> 1½ teaspoons mace
> ⅛ teaspoon powdered alum[4]

---

[4]Alum can be purchased in your local drugstore.

Burn a quarter teaspoon at a time on a hot charcoal. This incense stores well if it is kept in a closed bottle. It should be burned alternately with one of the spiritual incenses, or the vibration of the room where it is burned may become a bit too heavy.

This incense should not be used to cense people, as it has too heavy a vibration. For the same reason it should not be used for fumigations.

HOUSE BLESSING INCENSE

When you move into a new house you often want it to get a "homey" feeling quickly. This incense will assist in making your house into a home. It was devised by an expert in ceremonial magic,[5] and has been used by a number of people with success, including myself.

The incense improves with age, but it should be stored in a covered bottle. Mix this incense in the mortar and form into pills about the size of a pea.

      1 teaspoon powdered camphor gum
      1 teaspoon powdered nutmeg
      1 teaspoon powdered dried myrtle leaves

This incense may be burned in a censer, but the best way to use it to put a strong vibration in a new home is to arrange several incense burners throughout the house. You can use catfood cans and saucers for this, with a charcoal on each one. Place two pea-sized lumps or about an eighth teaspoon of incense on each charcoal. Let the fumes rise and permeate the whole house until there are no more fumes rising. This takes about an hour. As the scent is a bit strong, you may wish to air out the house afterwards, but the vibration will remain in the house.

A single application of this incense is sufficient. It will establish a good vibration throughout the entire house, and unless there is a traumatic upset, it will remain.

---

[5]David Conway, *Magic: An Occult Primer* (NY: Dutton, 1972) p. 97.

INCENSE FOR ABUNDANCE AND PROSPERITY IN THE HOME

Once you have established a good homey vibration in your house you might wish to refresh this vibration from time to time. Regularly used, say every month or so, the following incense will assist you in that effort. It has the quality of bringing abundance into your home, and when it is used as a censing incense throughout the house—with a prayer of thanksgiving—it will maintain the beneficial vibrations of the home and keep prosperity flowing in. This incense has other beneficial qualities as well, in that it has a spiritualizing effect in the place where it is burned. This assists in removing negative thoughtforms and keeping the home elevated.

In the mortar mix the following;

> 2 parts ground cinnamon
> 1 part nutmeg
> 1 part benzoin
> 1 part ground dried myrtle leaves

Burn about an eighth of a teaspoon at a time on a hot charcoal in a censer. Carry the censer with you as you move throughout the house, allowing the fumes to reach through the entire house. The remaining incense may be stored away in a closed bottle.

FUMIGATION WITH INCENSE

Fumigation is the process of using incense on a person, place, or thing to change the vibration of whatever is fumigated. The desire of the fumigation is to permanently change the vibration for the better. In the case of the fumigation of people, however, the change in the vibration is rarely lasting. Buildings and furniture will have a permanent change in vibration if they are thoroughly fumigated.

You might compare the concept of fumigation with the use of perfume. When you use any kind of scent you have a change in your vibration, but the change is not lasting because the scent wears off. You will experience a similar change as a result of using a fumigation. In the case of a fumigation, however, you will find that the change in the vibration is more subtle. It will take a few days or a week for your natural vibration to completely supersede the vibration placed on you by the fumigation.

The primary object of a fumigation, whether of a person, place, or thing, is to eliminate negative influences which may be present. This is the reason why knowing landlords have houses and apartments fumigated after a tenant leaves. The fumigation completely removes the vibration of the previous tenants and places a new vibration into the living space. The fumigation of a person has the same effect – first it cleanses them of negative influences, and second, it raises his or her vibration to a higher level.

When you fumigate a building it is necessary to use a number of incense burners. You may want to place one in every room of the house. A cleansing incense is placed on the coals of the incense burners and left for an hour or so. Once the cleansing is accomplished, the new vibration is placed in the building by burning a spiritual incense. You might want to use Coffee Incense to clean out the negativity in the place and then follow with House Blessing Incense to place a good vibration in the place.

When a crime of violence or murder has taken place in a house or apartment, it is frequently necessary to use incenses as well as other things to clean out the living quarters. Some of the materials used can be dangerous, so this type of cleansing is best left to those who have been trained to do it. One incense commonly used for this type of cleansing actually destroys the astral fabric in an apartment or house. With this type of cleansing the most evil vibrations can be removed and replaced with a feeling of sweetness and light.

Fumigating a person is a very simple thing, and one which will be found to be beneficial under all circumstances. You should get into the habit of using a fumigation on yourself whenever you still feel "grungy" after taking a cleansing bath.[6] The incense will remove astral forms which the bath will not. This is not because the incense is more effective than the bath, but simply that the incense removes one thing while the bath removes something else.

When you are fumigating yourself, you should avoid experimenting with incenses other than those given below. You are working with your personal vibration when you do a fumigation, and you may create a change that you will not like. After any fumigation, the effect will stay with you for at least twenty-four hours!

To fumigate yourself (or another person) you will need a straight-backed chair, a white sheet, your incense burner and the incense you have selected. Place the incense burner under the chair and light the charcoal. Place the incense on the hot charcoal and sit on the chair (either nude or in your underwear). Now gently wrap the sheet around you, covering the chair, and everything but your head. Be careful not to let the sheet hit the incense burner or the hot charcoal! Sit like this for ten or fifteen minutes and you will fumigate yourself very well indeed.

Allspice: Will assist you in being more harmonious with others. It is a good fumigation when you have difficulties in a marriage or at work.

Benzoin: Will assist in removing blockages to your growth. For spiritual assistance, it should be accompanied by a sincere prayer to God for help.

Cinnamon: Will assist you in gaining protection from outside forces, and from malicious or negative people. It can be used with a prayer for a job or a business opportunity.

Cloves: This is the best protective incense for fumigation. It will protect you from those who are deliberately malicious as well as from the sub-conscious negative thoughts of others. A

---

[6]For more information on this, see *Spiritual Cleansing*, pages 33 to 38.

clove fumigation is about the strongest protection fumigation there is.

Coffee: A good fumigation against negative entities, including the spirits of the dead. It is also a good fumigation for those who are sick or who have been sick for a period of time. It will remove heavy thoughtforms from people. It also puts an end to nightmares induced by heavy thoughts of yourself or others. Use regular ground coffee, not instant or decaffeinated coffee.

Frankincense: A general fumigation for cleansing and spiritual growth. It will assist you to get off on the right foot in any form of spiritual growth or exercise. It is probably the best general fumigation to start with.

Garlic Skins: The outer covering of the garlic is peeled off and discarded when you cook with garlic. The skins are good for the removal of negative thoughtforms or obsessive thoughts. You should fumigate yourself with garlic skins if you feel discouraged about something, or if one thought preys on your mind. After breaking off an affair, it is a good idea to fumigate yourself with garlic skins every week for the first month or so. This keeps thoughts of loss from becoming too strong.

Tobacco: Tobacco is an herb of Mars, and is often used in incense in small quantities to add the Mars vibration. It is good for physical protection and for freeing yourself from influences sent to you. It may also be used with a sincere prayer to free yourself of the ability to send the evil eye to others. There is enough tobacco in a cigarette to fumigate yourself.

5 Spells Using Oils

Oils are similar to water in that they have more effect on our emotional nature. Oils contain some of the earth element, so they effect the physical nature as well. Oils can be either of animal, mineral, or plant origin. Mineral oils have more of the earth quality in them, and are more suited to spells which fulfill earthly desires and negative magic. Plant oils carry with them the "feeling" or vibration of the plant from which they came. Animal oils also carry the vibration of their origin, but they are rarely found except in lard from the pig, and tallow from the sheep. Because animal oils affect the animal nature directly, they have developed a reputation in negative magic.

When you make up an oil you must remember that you are mixing the influence of the oil and the herb (or other material) you add to it. This requires a subtle ability to blend the vibrations correctly, and this only comes with experience. You are better off beginning with oils where the formula specifies the particular oil to be used. As with other magical spells, it does not pay to experiment until you can tell what you will have before you mix it.

There are a number of plant oils which can be used as a basis for magical oils. The following list gives some of the more commonly found oils and their uses. These oils can be purchased in health food stores or some of the larger grocery stores. For the most part, they are the oils most commonly used in magical work, primarily because they are easily available.

Almond Oil: This oil is said to correspond to the Sun in Leo. This kind of correspondence is found in a number of oils, and seems to be based on the fact that oils of all sorts were used in lamps in ancient times. The primary indicator of light is the Sun in Leo, so this attribution was given to many of these oils. I was originally taught that the almond was pre-eminently a plant of Venus, and that the virtue (or power) of Venus permeated all parts of the tree, including the oil. This coincides with the idea prevalent in most Western magic that the almond and the oil of the almond are the nut and oil of first choice for love spells or amatory magic. Almond oil is also useful for the restoration of health and mental stability. It is an excellent base for healing and massage oils.

In the East, among the Hindus, almond oil is used to promote chastity. The eating of almonds is undertaken for the same reason. This is an example of the differences in the beliefs of two cultures, and the way in which what you believe affects the results you obtain from the same ingredient. Obviously, if the oil can be used in love and sex spells it can also be used in chastity spells. The same force of the universe is present, and in this case the polarity of the force is chosen by the beliefs of the person using the oil.

Olive Oil: Also corresponds to the Sun in Leo. You will find that olive oil forms the base for most of the oils which originate in the Mediterranean area. This is simply because it is the most common cooking and lamp oil found there. Olive oil is a good base oil for all positive work. It is used for spells from gambling to love and everything in between. It is particularly good for spiritual or religious work, as it receives and holds a magical charge with little difficulty. It has a naturally clear vibration, which is not subject to decay. For this reason olive oil is difficult to use in negative work or in laying curses. Olive oil is the base oil for most of the Christian "anointing oils."

Soybean Oil: This oil is used in Chinese magical work, but I have never heard of it being specifically used as a magic oil. Perhaps some more knowledgeable reader will enlighten me.

Sunflower Oil: Also corresponds to the Sun in Leo. As the sunflower takes even its name from the Sun, it has a better chance of filling the correspondence than most of the other oils. Sunflower oil is used for much the same things as is olive oil. It is particularly good as a healing oil, and it works well as a massage or anointing oil. Sunflower oil has the ability to add "heat" to the body when used as a massage oil. This is not the heat of the menthol-based liniments, but the more subtle heat of the warmth of the sun and the life force.

Peanut Oil: This oil has a strong earth vibration. It is useful in magic as a healing oil, for money, employment, or for any form of earth magic. Peanut oil may be prayed over for the restoration of energy and vitality, and used as either a massage oil or as an anointing oil for this purpose. This is a useful bath oil for older people: a teaspoon to a tub of water is sufficient. There are better bath oils available commercially, however.

Mineral Oil: The oil commonly sold in supermarkets and drug stores is a petroleum product. It contains the virtue of the earth, but because it is a refined product of petroleum (much like vasoline, fuel oil, or even gasoline), it is used magically for its earthy vibration.

MAKING MAGIC OILS

Magic oils may be made from any plant or spice. They may also be made from other things, such as insects, stones or almost any other material desired. These oils all are a blend of the virtues of the oil and the material from which the oil is made.

To make any magic oil you need two clean bottles of approximately the same size. Wide mouth mason jars are best. Fill one of the bottles with the fresh or dried herbs from which you desire to extract the virtue. If you use fresh herbs, fill the entire bottle. Mash them up a bit, but do not pulverize fresh herbs. If you use dried herbs, fill the bottle about half full. Now pour in enough oil to cover the herbs. Cap the bottle tightly and place the bottle in a dark storage place for a week or two.

After one or two weeks have passed, fill the second bottle in the same way you filled the first one. You should use the same kind of herbs as you used with the first bottle. You should now pour the oil from the first bottle over the herbs in the second bottle. Allow all of the oil to drain from the first bottle. Again, store the bottle away for a week or two. The first batch of herbs may be discarded.

After another week or two have passed (or three to six weeks after you started the project), the oil is poured off into a clean bottle that it is to be stored in. It is now ready for your use. Again, the herbs are discarded. Some people like to keep at least some of the herbs in the bottle. If you wish to do so go right ahead. Others like to strain the oil by passing it through a cheesecloth filter. Either method is fine, as the oil will still have the virtue of the herbs. The process of the oils receiving the virtue of the herbs takes place while the herbs and oil are stored away for the "waiting period."

Be sure and label the bottles of finished oil, and also label the bottle of herbs you are storing away while they are ageing. You should keep your oils and the mixtures of herbs and oils out of the reach of children and curious adults.

When you make oils from dried ingredients it is a good idea to shake the bottle every day to promote a more intimate contact between the herbs and the oil. This will allow the oil to receive more of the virtue of the herbs than if it just sits. You will find that it is better to use fresh herbs in your oils, but as they are sometimes unavailable, the dried herbs will do well.

SOLARIZED OILS

In the section on water there was a fairly long explanation of the uses of solarized water. Oils may be exposed to the sun in the same way that waters can. From personal experience I can testify that solarized sunflower oil is an excellent massage oil for healing muscle cramps and infirmities. If you try making solarized oil, set a pint of sunflower oil on an east windowsill so that it is exposed between sunrise and noon on the day following the new moon in Leo. If you wish, you can pray over the oil before you place it on the windowsill, for your prayer will assist the oil in gaining energy for its work.

Solarizing other oils is much a matter of preference. Should you wish to make an oil for your skin, for example, you might wish to solarize some oil at the new moon in Libra. Peanut oil seems to be the best for this, but there is some debate on the matter. One woman I know swears by the almond oil she solarizes for her own use every year.

You can solarize herbal oils for better mixing of the virtues if you wish. The best rule I have found in this regard is simply to follow the formula for any oil until you really understand just how it works.

OIL SAMPLER

The following oils are basic ones that are frequently used. You will probably find you have a different set of favorite oils, but as a start you might make up these oils to keep on hand. They are fairly simple oils whose major function is in healing. Please note that these oils are for external application only, none of them are to be taken internally. They should all be labeled clearly and kept out of reach of children and curious adults.

Basil and Almond Oil: This oil is made with fresh basil. Steep the herb with almond oil for at least two weeks. The oil is a useful massage oil for general female complaints, lower back pain, or menstrual cramps. It is massaged on the abdomen or lower back in these cases. It can also be used as a candle oil when a woman is looking for a lover or a husband.

Clove and Sunflower Oil: This oil is best when made with a tablespoon of whole cloves and an eighth of a teaspoon of ground cloves. You should use about a pint of sunflower oil to cover the cloves, and then replace the cloves after the oil sits for two weeks.

    The clove/sunflower oil is good for massaging men. It will work well with general male complaints, including stiff backs. It is also a good candle oil for men in general, and is of some assistance to men who are looking for lovers, but there are better love spells for men than this one. The oil can help you protect yourself from negativity, however, and this is accomplished by placing a small dab of the oil over the breastbone after your morning shower.[1] This oil may be solarized. If you place it in the sun for a few days it seems to make a better blend—to be more "vital." I placed it in a south window after the new moon in Leo and left it for three days while on the second mix of the cloves and oil. I am quite pleased with the result.

Peanut Oil with Cloves/Benzoin: This is also a very protective blend. It is made in a manner similar to the clove/sunflower oil. Here you use peanut oil, and mix it with a pinch of ground benzoin, a tablespoon of whole cloves, and an eighth of a teaspoon of ground cloves. The result is an excellent and protective massage oil. Like the other oils, it is also good for a candle oil, and it seems to work well as a general purpose candle anointing oil.

---

[1]Women should use cinnamon and olive oil.

There is a variety of colors and scents which you can add to your oils. Some stores sell "do it yourself" perfume kits and colors and scents may be added to the above oil if you desire. I used a yellow color with a mixed floral scent for peanut oil and gave it to a friend as a gift. Green color combined with a rose scent seems to make the basil/almond oil more acceptable to women to use as a massage healing oil.

A bit of experimentation is worth while if you decide to add colors and scents to oil. You might bear in mind that green seems to relate to health for most people, while red relates to love and vigor. Yellow seems to stimulate the mental processes while blue is calming. Scents are very much a personal preference, the use usually depending on what you like. Remember that the food coloring colors which work so well with water do not work at all with oils! The same goes for scents. It takes special oil-based scents to blend with oils. Experiment, but be prepared to discard a lot of unsuitable oils. You will certainly learn from the experimentation.

HOLY ANOINTING OIL

One of the most popular anointing oils has a biblical origin. This is the Holy Anointing Oil (or Moses Oil) found at Exodus 30:23-33. The original version calls for more oil than one could use in several lifetimes. The version presented here is similar to the formula from the Old Testament. This blend yields a fine anointing oil which is suitable for blessing and other work. However, it is not subject to the prohibitions mentioned in the Bible.

To make this oil you should combine the following ingredients:

5 teaspoons powdered myrrh
2½ teaspoons powdered cinnamon
2½ teaspoons powdered sweet calamus
5 teaspoons powdered cassia

Place in a two quart bottle and shake the dry ingredients together until they are well mixed. Then pour in a quart of pure olive oil and shake again. Place in the window or some other sunny place for a month or six weeks before the summer solstice. To ensure a good blend it should be shaken well at least every three days or so.

At the summer solstice or shortly thereafter the oil should be filtered, placing the oil in small covered bottles. The spices used may then be thrown out.

Cinnamon used in this oil should be purchased from someone who can guarantee that it is true cinnamon, as the Food and Drug Administration allows cassia to be sold as cinnamon. Pure Saigon cinnamon is best for this oil. If possible, purchase the ingredients from a herb and spice store that knows its sources.

The oil should be prayed over before each use. It will take the energy of a blessing very well and it is particularly good for blessing people after cleansings.

Blessing Oil

A Blessing Oil is similar to an anointing oil. It is used to carry the force of the blessing given it when it is prayed over, and it imparts that blessing to the person who is to receive it. The following is one of the finest general blessing oils which can be made. It has been used successfully to lighten and elevate people, places, and things. The oil itself has a naturally high vibration, and when it is prayed over this vibration is modified successfully by the energy of the prayer.

Take one pint of pure olive oil and add:

> 1 teaspoon lotus root powder
> 1/4 teaspoon orris root powder

Shake together vigorously and place in the sunlight for a month. For best results you should shake the bottle every day to allow the ingredients to mix thoroughly. After a month it may be strained for use. If you wish you can keep the powders in the bottle, but some people find this unattractive. Remember to label the bottle and keep it out of reach of children and curious adults.

To bless someone, place a dab of oil on your finger and pray over it for the blessing which you wish to impart. Then apply the oil to the person to bless him or her. You can apply the oil wherever you wish to impart blessing – head, sternum, hands, etc.

Magnet Oil

Magnet oil or lodestone oil is used to draw things toward you. It carries the vibration of the magnet or lodestone and thus attracts things. You can find this oil in many occult or spiritual stores, but you will probably find your homemade product will work better.

You can make up a lifetime supply of magnet oil by placing a pint of mineral oil in a clear quart bottle with a wide mouth. A mason jar is fine for this purpose. Now add seven lodestones, one for each day of the week. (You can purchase lodestones at scientific supply stores, occult shops and some herb stores.) Lastly, add a quarter teaspoon "magnetic sand," or iron filings. You are now ready to energize the magnet oil. Place the bottle in an east window or in some place where it can catch the light of the rising sun for a week or so. You can gently swish the bottle every evening to mix the ingredients thoroughly, but don't shake it as the lodestones may cause the bottle to break.

After sitting in the window for a week, you can transfer the oil to smaller amber bottles for use. The bottles should then be placed in a dark place, hidden away. Be sure that you label the bottles, as the oil has no smell or taste to show what it is, and the vibration is usually not one you will be able to identify without a bit of concentration.

To increase your money supply you might want to use magnet oil to draw money toward you. You could do this by placing a bit of magnet oil on your money before you spend it. This will act to help the money return to you. To do this, you place a drop of magnet oil on your thumb and rub it out so that the tip of your thumb is covered with it. Now rub your thumb across all of the bills in your pocket, with a prayer that your money draw more money to you as you spend it.

Should you wish to draw a particular person into your life, you can use magnet oil to assist you in accomplishing this. You will have to take other steps as well, but the magnet oil can help. You should anoint the corners of a photograph of the person with a bit of the magnet oil, with the intention that you be able to meet the person under favorable circumstances.

Magnet oil can be used to anoint candles, and can be added to charms. You should always bear in mind that its principle is to draw things to you.

6 *Spells Using Herbs*

An herb is a plant you are familiar with while a weed is a plant you do not know how to use. The plant kingdom is full of all kinds of plants that are intimate with the forces of divine creation.

The influences of various plants can be sorted in many ways—on the Tree of Life, according to astrological rulerships, or any number of methods. However, it is important to understand that classifications of usefulness are not intrinsic to the plants themselves. Plants fulfill a place in the Divine Scheme without attempting to block the will of their creator.

This chapter presents a variety of herbal spells. They are taken from many different occult or spiritual practices and they demonstrate the various ways plants may be used in magic.

ADAM AND EVE ROOT

Adam and Eve root (also known as putty root) is found in the southern United States. It has been used for many years as a love charm by blacks in the south. It is under the general rulership of Venus, with a secondary influence from Saturn. Today the root is usually purchased as a curio in occult or herb and spice shops.

As a love charm it is usually made in pairs, one for each partner. The two roots are prayed over and one is given to each party in the relationship. The roots may be carried in a "charm bag" or otherwise carried on the person. This love charm is usually used when children are desired from the relationship; it is not used for casual affairs.

Adam and Eve root may also be used as a good luck charm, but it does not combine well with other ingredients in magical operations. As a good luck charm it is simply prayed over and given to the recipient to carry. Some people prefer it to any other charm you could make.

AGRIMONY

Agrimony (sometimes called cocklebur) is best known as a pesky weed which attaches itself to human and beast. It is very popular in folk healing, and less used in magic. Its many benefits in herbal medicine have earned for it the rulership of Jupiter, although some people feel it is ruled by Mars or Saturn. It has a curious property in magical application which makes it unique among herbs because this herb can assist you in releasing fears.

Occasionally a bit of agrimony is added to a charm bag to release fear. The charm can also be carried on your person, or a few burrs may be made into tea, which is added to a ritual bath. In cases where frightful events have taken place, some agrimony may be burned as an incense to remove the fear vibration from the location. It will release unconscious fears which you may not be able to admit you have.

If the debilitating fear is actually a belief, the cure is much slower than if the fear is a simple one which you have not fully accepted. A belief takes a long time to release, and should be handled consciously as well as magically.

Agrimony is used to break the most common curses, those which you impose on yourself through fear or guilt.

ALOE

Aloe is the holy herb of Islam, as rue is the herb of Christianity and hyssop the herb of Judaism. Moslems who have made the pilgrimage to Mecca hang aloe over their doorways as a protective measure, and as a symbol of their pilgrimage.

The herb itself is a symbol of patience, especially the patient submission to the will of God. It may be used in baths to assist the development of patience in people. Use about a quarter cup of chopped aloe, which can be steeped in a quart of boiling water. Add to a tub of water, and soak in the bath fifteen to twenty minutes.

Aloe has many uses in medicine as well. It is a particularly soothing herb which is used to heal cuts and abrasions.

ASAFETIDA

Used in Indian culinary feasts, curries, and so forth it is called "the food of the gods." To those of us who dislike the smell, it is called "Devil's Dung." Asafetida is a pasty, granular, and odorous compound.

Asafetida is burned as an incense in rites of negative magic. Compounded with sulfur it is said to summon the spirits of hell. It has the property of attracting negative and malicious spiritual entities. Over the years it has become a favorite of the Christian Satanists, who seem to think that it does what it promises.

This is an example of an incense which can get one into a good deal of trouble, and is best avoided. Those who are wise will avoid it; those who are not can use it to harm themselves.

BASIL

In the Middle Ages, basil was classed as an herb of Mars. It was said that if basil were crushed it would breed scorpions. At the same time, it was considered to be a divine herb, and supposedly it brought good fortune to the place where it was kept. It is certainly one of the most useful herbs in herbal magic.

Basil is used as a spray or a sprinkle to clear or lighten the place where it is placed. It is used in the corners of sick rooms, as a floor wash, and as a house sprinkle.

A teaspoon of basil added to a bottle of ethyl rubbing alcohol will make an excellent neck and shoulder rub for the relief of tension caused by the working day. Used in a bath, a tea made of a teaspoon of basil steeped in a cup of boiling water has a protective and cleansing influence. It is particularly useful to clean off the feelings left by contact with those who are negative or controlling.

The tobacco from a cigarette and as much basil, burned on charcoal, will provide a simple incense which will drive away negative influences from the place where it is burned. In all cases, basil is protective of the place where it is used.

BAY LEAF

The "noble laurel" is best known for its use in cooking meats. It has the reputation of being a hallucinogenic herb, as it was regularly chewed by the prophetic priestesses of the Oracle at Delphi. It also formed the "laurel crown" of poets and philosophers.

Magically, bay leaf is used for granting wishes. There are a number of forms of this spell, but the following is the simplest and most effective. It, like other wish spells, is based on the concept that if you really know what you want you can have it.

Write the wish out on a piece of paper. Fold the paper into thirds, and place three bay leaves inside. Again fold the paper into thirds, and put it away in a dark place. Once the wish is granted the paper should be burned as a thank you. The process of writing out the wish, and folding the paper, must be done while concentrating on the wish.

BLESSED THISTLE

The blessed thistle, or holy thistle, has a long history as a good luck charm. It may either be carried on your person or placed in your house to attract good luck. In the house it can be used in an arrangement of dried flowers in the main room. Occasionally it is placed in an arrangement by itself.

The blessed thistle is able to absorb negative influences, and this is what gives it its reputation as a good luck charm. If you decide to place some blessed thistle in your home, you might wish to change them every week or so, as they absorb their limit of negativity in that time.

BROOM TOPS OR BROOM HERB

The use of broom herb in a bath is mentioned in the chapter on water and baths. Broom herb is very useful as a washing compound. It may be used to clear away any astral detritus from floors, walls, and furniture. A cup or two of broom tea per bucket is all that is required. The mop or scrub sponge should be rinsed in another bucket to get the best cleansing effect.

Cool broom tea can be prayed over to make a protective sprinkle for the home. It is not particularly effective as a protection, and does much better in cleansing.

Loose broom herb, placed in the corners of a room, can keep the astral environment of the room clean. The herb should be changed every week or so, as it has little staying power. Fresh broom herb is best for this use.

CARDAMOM

Cardamom is a popular spice—it is used to flavor coffee in Arabic countries; Scandinavian recipes call for it in baking; it is used to flavor meet in curries. In magic it is primarily used as an incense to calm the place where it is burned. Cardamom is not a good herb for baths, as it has only a temporary effect on the emotions, and, although it can balance the person, the effect is brief. As a calming incense, it's particularly useful for the consultation room.

CHESTNUT

Chestnut trees belong to Jupiter. As all nuts or fruits of plants relate to Jupiter, the nuts of the chestnut tree have a very strong power of Jupiter. They may be used (raw, not roasted) in a charm bag to add the virtue of Jupiter, and they expand any quality which the charm bag already has.

The nuts may be used in a bath to gain the virtue of Jupiter, for example, in assisting a woman to become pregnant. Five nuts (five being the usual number of Jupiter) should be used in the bath.

Chestnuts are a poor choice for the usual novice desire of drawing money, as the Jupiter vibration will usually encourage the individual to spend money rather than to acquire it. One nut, or a necklace of them, may be prepared as a charm for money, however. The prayer for a charm that includes chestnut should limit the time element involved, or the prayer will be too general to be of real effect.

It can also be prepared as a charm to place under the chair in the consultation room, to encourage clients to be generous, a practice that may fall into the realm of black magic!

CHEWING JOHN

Chewing John is so called because of its use as a chewing root. It can be chewed when you seek good fortune, or for its spicy taste. It adds a nice flavor to rice. Chewing John is often made into a good luck charm, being prayed over and carried on your person or in a charm bag.

The root finds its best use as a money drawing charm. It is placed in a chamois skin charm bag with three silver coins, usually dimes. The root will receive the influence of the prayer prayed over it very well, and it seems to act to open up opportunities for money to come. It can be used to make up an attractive charm, but as silver is more expensive now it is not always an easy charm to make.

The powder is one of the best casting powders (or "persuasion" or "compelling" powders) there is for sex. It should be prayed over and touched to the body of the person you desire to have sex with. It is not a "love powder," it is strictly a "sex" powder.

CINNAMON

Cinnamon is one of the most useful spices in magical practice. It is used for purification, blessing, protection, and prosperity. It is a primary ingredient in many of the powders and incenses used in both Eastern and Western magical practices. True cinnamon powder should be purchased from an herb store, as the grocery store product is usually cassia, an entirely different thing altogether. The Food and Drug Administration allows cassia to be labeled as cinnamon, so it takes a bit of searching to find the real thing.

Cinnamon is perhaps most useful in protecting yourself from the envy and jealousy of others. Using it is simplicity itself: simply place a dab of cinnamon, about half as much as will cover the head of a match, on your breastbone while you are dressing.

You can also mix it with plain unscented talcum powder. A half teaspoon cinnamon to two cups of talcum powder will give you a good mixture. This talcum may be used as a dusting powder after the bath, and the protective influence of cinnamon will surround you.

CINQUEFOIL

Cinquefoil (also known as Five Finger Grass) is used as an ingredient in many charm bags, or as a charm by itself. It has the ability to make you speak eloquently, to the best of your ability. It acts to stimulate the memory and allow words to flow. A bath for this purpose is useful, for example, just before an employment interview. A teaspoon of cinquefoil to a cup of boiling water will make the solution for the bath.

Cinquefoil can also be used to make people speak their minds, not always the wisest thing to do. The name of the individual who is to speak should be written on a piece of paper, and cinquefoil herb placed over it. The paper is then prayed over for the effect desired. This is an excellent way to get a witness to testify in court, for he or she usually says more than necessary and in some cases it is difficult to get the witness to shut up.

DEVIL'S SHOESTRINGS

Devil's shoestrings is an aptly named herb, as anyone who has tried to clear it from a garden patch will testify. It is famed for its persistence, and its ability to add a "staying quality" to whatever it is used in. The herb itself will take a strong charge from the prayer made over it, and it will act with the same persistence that it displays in the garden.

The most famous spell which uses this herb is the "compelling spell," which is used to gain agreement from another person. It is often used by people who have to negotiate, and it has an excellent reputation for success. The spell must be made for the person who is going to use it, and prayed over in that person's name.

Pieces of devil's shoestrings are cut about one and a half to two inches long, and placed into a wide mouthed bottle. Several lumps of camphor are added, and the bottle is filled with bourbon whiskey. The filled bottle is then prayed over in the name of the person who is to use it. The bottle is then capped and stored in a dark place.

To use the spell, a piece of the root is taken from the bottle and rubbed between the hands. The root is then returned to the bottle, and the person using the spell simply shakes hands with the person he or she wishes to influence.

FENUGREEK

Fenugreek is one of our oldest cultivated plants. It is used as a food in many parts of the world, and as a condiment or seasoning in others. In ancient Egypt it was used as a part of the Kuphi incense, the Holy Smoke which was burned as an offering to the gods.

Fenugreek is still used as an ingredient in incense in some practices today, but its most common use is as a headwash. Tea of Fenugreek is allowed to cool and the head washed thoroughly with it. Let the residue stay on the head for twenty-four hours, and wash it off the following day. This has a clearing effect on the head, and is specifically recommended for improving clarity of thought. Use this headwash on those days when you feel dull, afflicted or muddle-headed – it's a sure way to get your clarity back. It also works to destroy any thoughts which are being sent you by others. You might try it when you find yourself having strange and usually negative thoughts about yourself.

GARLIC

Garlic is a hardy perennial with long, flattened, solid leaves. The bulb, the part most used, is composed of several smaller sections known as "cloves." The whole bulb is covered with a membranous skin. Garlic has been used throughout history as a medicinal and a food and has been credited with almost magical properties in curing disease. It is used in magic in numerous ways, and it has been a religious offering since Egyptian times.

Garlic is the exemplar of plants in its astrological response. It is very strongly aligned with Mars in Aries, and is used as an offering to the warrior deities in most pantheons. It is also used to remove the evil eye, and to take aggressive action against enemies.

To keep money in the house, burn the skin covering the garlic cloves in the kitchen fire. Or burn it on a charcoal if you have an electric stove.

Dried ground garlic is often used in incense to remove heavy thoughtforms, negative entities and thoughts of depression. A blend of dried and powdered garlic and onion powders is effective for these purposes, but the area should then be infumed with a lighter incense, such as frankincense, to neutralize the heavy Mars influence of the garlic and onion mixture. Garlic and brown sugar mixed with benzoin in equal quantities is a useful incense for purifying and cleansing the inside of a building. It is especially effective in the rooms of someone who lives in a state of depression. It lightens the living quarters considerably.

Garlic can also be used in baths for personal protection. Boil nine cloves of garlic in an iron (or stainless steel) pot with about a quart of water. Boil for about twenty minutes, allow the solution to cool to room temperature. Take a regular cleansing bath, with soap and water, then pour the garlic solution over your head. Allow the solution to run out the bath drain while praying that evil be washed off. This bath is effective against most negative influences, and is very good against the physical debilitation brought on by the evil eye or consistent negativity from others.

Three garlic cloves in a red charm bag is considered to be a very useful charm against the evil eye. Garlic is also the traditional protection against vampires.

Garlic has so many uses in folk healing that there have been several books written on the subject. Crushed garlic is occasionally rubbed on the feet to reduce fever. There is also a prayer to St. Ajo (St. Garlic) for healing – an indication of how powerful garlic is thought to be in medicine.

Garlic grows wild almost everywhere. I have found garlic plants in New York's Central Park and in vacant lots and fields in the city. I have also found it growing along the roadways of Pennsylvania and New Jersey. It is certainly one of the most interesting magical and culinary herbs in the world.

GINGER

It is the root of the ginger plant that we know as ginger and this is the part used – either whole, fresh, dried or powdered. Ginger has been used as a culinary spice since 550 B.C., and is particularly prevalent in Chinese cooking.

This herb relates to Mars, but it is the *active* Mars, and is quite different from the Mars in Aries vibration of garlic. Ginger is used as a catalyst, promoting a rapid change in conditions. If you add small quantities of ginger to any incense, it will enhance the effects of the incense and make it work more quickly.

Elementally, ginger is the "fire of air." It is used in spells of all kinds to assist them being brought to fruition more quickly. Take care that whenever ginger is used in a spell, it is the smallest of the components of the spell. If too much ginger is used, it will overwhelm the other components, making the spell a waste of effort.

GRAINS OF PARADISE

Grains of paradise are the guinea peppers of the East Coast of Africa. They are a prime constituent of African magical practice, as well as African food. They are used to feed the saints in some magico-religious practices. For this purpose they are placed in small charm bags and hung behind pictures of the saints on the walls of the home or on the home altar.

Grains of paradise are also added to red charm bags to "add power" to them. Seven grains, steeped in boiling water, are used to make a bath for men who are having trouble with gaining the affection of women. Three grains are used to gain a favorable judgment in court, but as the spell requires that they be prayed over and then placed on the desk of the judge, it is a bit difficult to accomplish in the modern courtroom.

Grains of paradise are also used as an incense to summon specific deities in some of the magico-religious practices of African origin. This use is not only a bit tricky, it is an initiatory use which is not possible for non-initiates to use safely. This is an example of how you can get yourself into a good deal of difficulty with too little knowledge.

HAZELNUT

The hazelnut is the Celtic nut of wisdom. It can be used by people who desire mental stability, calm, or insight into difficulties. A bath made with nine hazelnuts can assist in cleaning the mental body as well as stimulating the mind. The bath is made by boiling nine hazelnuts in an iron pot with a quart of water for an hour or so. Once the liquid cools it is added to a tub bath.

A necklace made from hazelnuts may be worn to gain the same effect, or to preserve the effect once the mental body has been cleaned. It will take several weeks for the necklace to have the proper effect, and it should be worn almost continuously during this time. Carrying a hazelnut in your pocket has almost no effect, as the vibration of the hazelnut is not particularly intense.

A tea made from nine hazelnuts will assist a business in obtaining customers. The tea is used to mop the cleaned floors of the business place and is made the same way you would make it for a ritual bath.

Adding ground hazelnut flour to foods may also assist the mental vibration, particularly if it has been prayed over.

HIGH JOHN THE CONQUEROR

High John the Conqueror (jalap) is one of the better known magical roots. It has been prepared and carried as a good luck charm for many years. It is one of the best known good luck charms, and its use dates from the days of slavery in the American South, where it was used and prepared by blacks. In the Gulta region of North Carolina, it is the subject of a number of stories which are legendary in nature. I have heard at least two versions of how an ancestor used the root to convince the "master" to set him free.

Because it is such a useful root, and because it is a basic part of most American magical practices, it will be used as an example of how a single herbal substance can be used in a number of ways. It is one of the most versatile magical substances available.

Making the Oil

Split four or five High John the Conqueror roots into small pieces. As it is a hard root, I recommend a chopping block and an axe. Place the pieces in a small bottle and cover them with olive oil (or cottonseed oil). For more negative work, mineral oil should be used. Place the bottle with the root pieces and the oil in the sunlight for at least a week, which allows the oil to absorb the virtue of the root pieces. You can either leave the root pieces in the oil or strain them out as you desire. As only a little of the oil is used at a time it is probably just as well to keep them in.

Making the Water

Boil four or five roots in an iron pot for a few hours. You will have to add water as the pot boils, for if the pan runs dry you will have to begin the process all over again. You should end up with about a pint of water and the roots. Throw away the roots and save the water. Add two or three shots of vodka to the water and store it away until you want to use it. It is better to store it in a dark place.

Making the Powder

File away the outer covering of the root with a wood rasp, and file as much of the powder as you desire. To keep the powder fresh you should only file as much as you are going to use at one time.

Using High John the Conqueror Root

The root, in whatever form you desire to use it, is a material which will change conditions. It has gained widespread reputation as a compelling material, to make another person succumb to the desires of the one using it. It may be used to gain love or money, but it is always used to influence another person to your advantage.

You can use the oil, by praying over it and putting it on someone. You can use the powder as a casting powder to be sprinkled over the doorstep of someone's house. The water can be used to wipe down a chair you know someone will sit in. In any of these cases you can have the other person at a disadvantage when dealing with you.

The disadvantage of the use of this root is that it must be prayed over for what you specifically want, in as much detail as you can think of. This means that you must know exactly what you want, without any obscurities or fudging. Once you know what you really want you are half way to having it in any event, with or without the use of magic.

HORSE CHESTNUT

The horse chestnut has an unusual property. It has the virtue of being able to absorb physical pain from those who carry it or apply it to themselves. It is very useful for people who suffer from arthritis or bursitis, and it is carried in purse or pocket to gain some relief. The nut should be prayed over in the name of the person before it is given to him or her.

A bowl of nuts, say three or four nuts in a small bowl, may be kept in the sickroom of a person who is in pain. The nuts should be prayed over in the name of the person, and then washed off in cool water every day to increase their ability to accept the pain. Once a nut used for this purpose becomes damaged—its skin cracks, for example—it should be discarded. It has done its work, and needs to be replaced.

HYSSOP

Hyssop is the holy herb of Judaism, just as rue is the holy herb of Christianity and aloe the holy herb of Islam. The use of hyssop in Jewish religious practice is described in Psalm 51: "Purge me with hyssop and I shall be clean." Hyssop was used as an aspergillum, to spread holy water around the temple. It still plays some part in the Jewish liturgy, as one of the herbs served at Passover.

Hyssop has a cleansing quality. It is used in baths for cleansing as well as a sprinkle for cleansing the home. It may also be used as a spray, to lighten the vibrations of a place. It can be used to mop a floor or rug (damp mop) to remove feelings of negativity which may be present.

Hyssop tea is made by adding a tablespoon of the herb to a cup of boiling water. Let the tea cool, and use it as you desire — as a ritual bath, a sprinkle, or whatever.

LOVAGE ROOT

Lovage is known as the "loving herb." In English folklore it is used to bring love to the person who uses it, and it has been used in a variety of ways to attract love. A bath may be made from a tablespoon of the ground root steeped in a cup of boiling water for this purpose. The resulting tea is added to the bath, and a prayer for a lover is made while bathing.

Lovage root can also be used in another kind of love spell, one more suited for marriage. The root is split open, and a piece of paper with the names of the two lovers is inserted into the root. The root is then tied, paper included, with three threads, one red, one green and one white. The completed packet is buried along the foundation wall of the house in which the two lovers live. The intention of the spell is to provide permanent love between the two people.

The white string or thread is for purity, to keep the lovers faithful to each other. The red is for mutual passion, while the green is for prosperity and offspring.

LOW JOHN

Low John is also known as ground thistle or southernwood. It can be used to reverse spells cast by others (see page 14). Low John is also used in love spells. Its influence is protective, and can be used for any other work being done, and added to charm bags for that purpose. Oil of bergmont is usually the preferred medium for love charms, but a piece of Low John has about the same influence as two or three drops of oil of bergmont.

Low John can also be used negatively. Placed over a doorway, for example, it makes negative influences more uncomfortable in the room. It can also be placed under a bed or sewn into a pillow, for the same purpose.

Low John is not a particularly good incense in my experience. If you use it, be sure to pray over it before you use it.

MARIGOLD

The marigold is not only a beautiful garden or house plant, it is one of the most potent plants used in magic. As a plant of both the Sun and the Moon, it has a host of useful magical properties. In the garden, it is planted as a border to protect plants and seedlings from insects. In herbal medicine it has been used for healing damaged flesh and open wounds. It is an herbal specific for cancers which are ulcerous, several cups of the tea being taken each day until the cancer is healed.

Magically, the tea made with a tablespoon of the flowers and a cup of water. It is an excellent condenser of the astral force. The tea may be placed in a charm bag and prayed over to keep the charm "on target," or a few drops of the tea may be prayed over and rubbed on the hands.

Magic mirrors may be made through the use of the alcoholic extract of the marigold flowers. The mirror is made by coating the front of a piece of cleaned window glass with the solution, and then it is prayed over to see what one wishes to view. If the glass is not cleaned, the astral charge will reveal itself constantly through such a mirror.

MARJORAM

Marjoram is the familiar kitchen herb. It is not used often in American cooking, and it is almost unknown in American magical practice. It does have a very interesting quality, however, which makes it worth mentioning. The herb can be used to clean negative thoughtforms out of a place by sprinkling it on the floor and sweeping the floor. The marjoram absorbs negativity, and is swept out of the house with it.

While a tea may be made from marjoram (a teaspoon of the chopped herb to a cup of boiling water), it is not as effective as the use of the herb as a sweeping compound. If you do not wish to use marjoram as a sweeping compound it may be used as an incense to rid a place of negativity, but it will work better as a sweeping compound.

MATE

The use of this herb in a cleansing bath is mentioned in the section on water and baths.

Mate is used as a magical powder to rid a person or thing of the influence caused by spirits of the dead. The fine powder is blessed, prayed over, and blown on the person to be cleansed. The influence will last as long as the powder remains on the person. In some of the Afro-Catholic magico-religious practices of South America, powdered mate and finely powdered eggshell are combined for this purpose.

The powder itself, or a tea made from the herb, can be used to reduce spirit influence in a place. The powder is placed in the corners of the room (or the corners of a drawer), while the tea is used to mop the floor. Add a cup or two of mate tea to a bucket of mop water.

A friend of mine places teabags of mate tea in the corners of his dresser drawers. I do not feel that spirits are that interested in laundry, but he thinks that there is some advantage to it. I would think that putting the herb in your pillow case would be more effective in reducing nighttime spirit activity in the bedroom.

MINT (SPEARMINT)

Mint has a quality which stimulates. It may be used to "spice up" charms to make them work faster, or to turn your mentality so you can be in accord with the effect desired from your charm. As a spray or sprinkle it puts a mentally stimulating vibration throughout the place where it is applied. It would be ideal for a school, but it is also useful in an office or a house that is for sale.

Mint may be used as a floorwash in a business place, to stimulate business activity. Honeysuckle and cinnamon do better here though.

If you rinse your hair with mint it will often remove minor mental dullness. Wash your hair and rinse it with a mint tea, made of a teaspoon of dried mint leaf to a cup of boiling water. Allow the water and mint to come to room temperature before you apply it to your head. When rinsing, scrub the scalp thoroughly. This is a first aid treatment for minor forms of malochia.

MUGWORT

Mugwort is one of those plants which is usually considered to be a weed. Since ancient times it has been considered a bringer of prophecy through dreams. As an incense it is believed to assist people in trance or when they are asleep to "dream true." For dreams you burn it as an incense in your bedroom before retiring, or you can make a mugwort "dream pillow," the more usual method of using the herb.

A mugwort "dream pillow" is made by filling a pillow case with mugwort leaves. You should sleep alone when you use it, and remember to have a pencil and paper at your bedside to write down any dreams that may come along.

MYRTLE

Myrtle is a component of a blend called Angel Water, which is made from myrtle tea, orange water and rose water. Myrtle is used to bring positive spirit influences to a place, but is not as effective as simply burning benzoin incense.

Myrtle is useful as a magical powder, for either casting or blowing. The powder takes a charge well and, depending on the prayer made over it, can be used to rapidly change conditions.

Myrtle does not work as well as an incense, but if a small amount is added to other incenses, the effect of the original blend is usually enhanced. Add only a very small amount, however. Too much will make the incense smell like burning leaves.

ORRISROOT

Orrisroot (also known as Queen Elizabeth root) is the root of the garden iris. It is a well known love charm, and is often carried by people who wish to draw love to themselves. It can be used in powder form to draw others to yourself. In this case it can be added to talcum powder as a dusting powder. Add a tablespoon of orris root powder to a cup of talcum powder; pray over it for the effect you desire. It can be used to draw others for business purposes or for romance.

The powder of the root relates to the planetary influence of Mercury, through the greek goddess Iris, a messenger of the gods. Orrisroot is a useful ingredient in any spell where communications or the opening of communications is desired. For this purpose it is added to charm bags or baths.

Occasionally orrisroot is used as a condiment in Europe. As such, it has the reputation of producing love between those who partake in the meal.

PARSLEY

Parsley is a beneficial herb for women. It can be made into a sprinkle which has the effect of calming and protecting the home. In a bath it gives benefit to people's financial problems. For either of the above, make a tea with a teaspoon of dried parsley to a cup of boiling water. Allow the tea to steep until the water reaches room temperature, and either add it to the bath or use it as a house sprinkle or spray. It may also be used as a floorwash if desired.

Some people avoid eating parsley, as it is supposed to confer financial benefit if one does not do so. The same is held to be true about pumpkins. This may be a superstition, but if one accepts it, it is as firm a belief as any other.

PEONY

The leaves and flowers of the common peony are used in washes and baths, particularly in initiatory practices. The root of the peony is used as a good luck charm, and is often added to charm bags for success and to reverse spells sent against the wearer.

The seeds of the Peony are considered to be very dangerous, as very powerful curses are placed with them. Peony seeds are said to cause disorder and strife when they are scattered in a room. The person who steps on a peony seed usually starts an argument with *the* one person in the room whom he or she should avoid in the first place!

The peony seed is the reputed Jumby Bean of folk magic, and its use in magic as an agent of cursing is well known.

POKE ROOT

This plant is also known as the ink-berry plant. The berries of this plant make a good red dye when crushed, and can be used as the "dove's blood ink" so beloved of occult supply stores. The root of the poke plant is used to break spells and curses. It should be boiled as a tea and added to the bath or scrub water. It is particularly effective immediately after the new moon. To use this bath effectively, first mop your floors, using a cup of poke root tea in a bucket of water. Then take the bath, adding a cup of the tea to your bath water. Any remaining tea can be sprinkled in the corners of the house.

Poke root has a strong influence on the astral condition, and it can be very effective for certain people who need stabilizing on their path in life. The well-dried root can be ground into an excellent magical powder, and can be used to place an influence on others to respect authority and straighten out their lives.

ROSEMARY

Rosemary is supposed to be used for remembrance. It is claimed that it improves the memory, and is used as a hair rinse for this purpose. For some time it has been used as a hair rinse for strictly cosmetic purposes, which seems to be a better use than trying to improve your memory with it.

In most magical practices, rosemary is used as a protective herb, or for purification of the ritual area, persons, places, and things. In some of the older witchcraft practices, rosemary is spread around the place to be protected before the ritual worship begins. Whole rosemary "needles" are used for this purpose.

Whole or powdered rosemary can be made into a tea, a teaspoon of the herb to a cup of boiling water steeped until it reaches room temperature. The tea is good for a purification bath for those suffering from bad vibes. It can also be used to rinse off furniture which is brought into the house after having been used by others.

When either the powder or the leaf (which is needle-like in shape) is placed in the corners of a room, it adds a protective feeling to the place. It is a good thing to use in a child's bedroom during the "terrible two" phase.

RUE

Rue is the "herb of grace" in the Christian religion. It holds a place like hyssop in Judaism and aloe in Islam, as the "holy herb" of the religion. Carrying a sprig of rue is supposed to protect the person from the influence of evil spirits.

Burned as an incense, rue is supposed to add virtue to a place and protect those who use it against temptation. In fact, it strengthens the willpower of people who are in the place where it is burned.

Rue has been used as an incense to drive away evil spirits and negative influences. It also has been used to attract money to the place where it is burned. In all cases it acts to strengthen the willpower of the person using it, and thus assists us in gaining our desires, whatever they are.

Rue is occasionally used to sprinkle Christian Holy Water around a place, or on a person. In this use it has as much virtue as the person using it thinks it has.

ST.-JOHNS-WORT

St.-Johns-wort has the reputation of being one of the most protective herbs there is. It has been used to "banish or drive away all phantoms, shades, spirits, and works of the devil." To use it for this remarkable purpose, simply hang the herb at the place where the negative forces are to be blocked. This could be at a window, a doorway, or even around the neck of a person.

St.-Johns-wort is named for John the Baptist, whose feast day occurred at the summer solstice in the old (Julian) calendar. It is from the power of this famous personage who not only baptized Christ, but founded his own religion (The Mandian, or River Brethren) that the power of the herb supposedly comes. As with most herbs however, it is the inherent virtue of the herb which has been adapted to suit the personages of the religious practice.

The Druids supposedly used St.-Johns-wort to remove astral influences from people before the time of Christ. The history of the herb in magic is certainly of greater date than the spell which attributes the herb to the Apostle John provided here. This prayer is to be recited as St.-Johns-wort is burned in the family fireplace, or used as an incense to fumigate the home.

> Saint John the Apostle of Christ
> Who was by Christ called the Beloved
> Be with all in this house,
> And through thy holy office,
> Drive away all phantoms, shades and spirits,
> Keep and protect us from the works of the devil,
> That thy grace, and the mercy of Christ
> Be with this house, and all in it,
> So long as this house shall stand.
> In the name of Christ Jesus,
> Through the Glory of St. John
> Amen.

This is an example of how a herb with a strong virtue—in this case for protection—can be adapted to suit the beliefs of many cultures over time. The above prayer came from a Pennsylvania hex-practitioner. I asked if the herb was named after St. John the Baptist, and he said, "No, why would they name the herb after him, and not the Apostle?"

SAGE

Sage is an herb of wisdom. It is used to bring problems or difficulties to resolution, to destroy illusions. A tea made from a teaspoon of sage and a cup of boiling water is added to a tub bath for this purpose. When the tea is sprinkled throughout a house it will increase the mental clarity of the occupants of the house.

Sage may be added to a charm bag to increase the potential for thought about the matter at hand. In this case it allows the owner of the charm to think more clearly about the matter, and with less illusions about it.

Mint, sage and cinquefoil are often combined to make a charm which causes the person using it to seem wise and trustworthy to others. The herbs are blended in equal quantities, and sewn up in a small white "pillow" of cotton cloth. This pillow is then prayed over for the effect desired, using the name of the one who is to use the charm. The completed charm is then placed in a small red charm bag and given to the recipient.

Sage, as an incense, can go both ways with ease. It is better to avoid using sage in incenses, and if it is decided to use it, always pray over it first for the effect desired.

SAMPSON SNAKEROOT

Sampson snakeroot is another useful herb which is usually treated as a garden pest. It is used in charms and has the reputation of aiding the restoration of male virility. For this purpose, a piece of the root is prayed over and worn around the neck. It should be worn for seven days before it is removed.

It is also thought that if a person chews the root he or she will be liked by others. In this case, several small pieces of the root are taken and are chewed "all day," one piece after another. By sunset the person is supposed to gain in popularity.

This herb has an antipathy to iron, so the pieces of root used should be broken off by twisting or biting, rather than cutting with a knife. Many herbs have various antipathies, such as "gather at the full moon," or "gather at night," and so on. It pays to experiment to see if these instructions are real, as many of them are not. The use of a knife on Sampson snakeroot debilitates its ability to accept the force of the prayer, which is a good reason to avoid cutting it.

SANDALWOOD

Sandalwood is the single most popular incense fragrance. It is so popular that it is sold throughout the world as an incense, primarily in the form of sticks. It is burned as an incense for all sorts of reasons.

In Oriental religious practice (the Chinese, Hindu, and Japanese religious pantheons) sandalwood is burned as an offering to deities. For this purpose it is prayed over and dedicated to the specific deity. Like any prayer to a deity, this should be done only if one has a connection with the deity.

Sandalwood incense is thought to be invigorating to the elemental spirits. These are the spirits of earth, air, fire, and water who act to manifest the physical world. Occasionally this connection is taken advantage of by making a prayer for something which is wanted in the life while burning the incense. If one has a strong natural connection with the elemental forces, as indicated, for example, by pointed ears like Dr. Spock, the prayer will probably work.

SOUTHERN JOHN THE CONQUEROR

Bethroot, better known as southern John the Conqueror, is an unusual looking root. It has a small solid body which is circled by tiny rootlets. It looks as if each of these rootlets was grasping, like a burr.

The root has been used as a money charm for many years. To make a most effective money charm from the root put it in a small bowl and pray over it, asking the root to bring in money. The bowl and root are placed in a dark place in the house, in a closet for example. Once a week, as long as the money supply is coming in, it is fed with a penny, by placing the penny in the bowl.

If you wish, you can pray over the root and put it in a charm bag. If it is carried on your person it will have the effect of opening up your personal money supply, but it is primarily a household money charm.

SOLOMON'S SEAL ROOT

Solomon's seal is well known as a magical plant. The root of the plant is ground and used as an incense in rituals. It is a good medium in rituals where you wish to summon a spirit to visible appearance. The fumes of the incense act as the body which the spirit forms itself around. Some fumes act better for this purpose than others – benzoin, for example, will provide a form for only the most elevated spirits, and is of little use to the average person. Solomon's seal root will provide a form for the vast majority of spirits, and will suit the spell-caster who works with a variety of spiritual intelligences.

Solomon's seal root provides an excellent wash for sacred areas – altars and so forth. The altars, walls, and floors of temples and ritual areas can be washed with a tea made by boiling a tablespoon of the root in a gallon of water for about twenty minutes. The solution is allowed to cool and is then strained through cheesecloth. The cleared liquid is added to the wash water, about a cup to a standard wash bucket. Preparing an area in this way will also assist in summoning to visible appearance.

TONKA BEAN

The tonka bean is a short blackish bean that vaguely looks like a small piece of a vanilla bean. It has a distinctive flavor and taste. In magical use, the bean has gathered a great reputation as a charm, being used both as a love charm, and to ward off the evil eye.

As a charm to attract love, it is simply carried in the pocket or worn in a charm bag. To ward off the evil eye it is placed on a necklace, or a number of beans may be strung on a necklace, and is worn around the neck. Bracelets may also be made from the tonka bean. They cast a protective vibration on the person who wears them.

VERVAIN

Vervain was known as the holy herb of the Druids, and was used for magic and medicine. It is most useful as a spray or a housecleaning herb, as it will remove heavy vibrations. It will bring peace and contentment, eliminating the more malicious thoughtforms.

The tea is made by steeping about a tablespoon of the herb in a cup of hot or boiling water. Once cool, the herb is strained out and the water is used as a spray, a sprinkle, or on a washcloth as a part of the housecleaning routine. This solution is also used to wash altars to remove heavy thoughtforms.

Burned as an incense, vervain will act to remove heavy and malicious thoughtforms. In the Middle Ages it was thought to drive out devils when it was burned in the fireplace. Vervain has so many herbal uses in magic that it is also known as the enchanter's herb.

The use of vervain as a sprinkle was known in ancient times. Both Pliny and Discordies wrote that "water in which vervain has been steeped, if it be sprinkled in a room will make the guests merrier."

WORMWOOD

Wormwood has long had a connection with the spirit forces. Historically, it has been used for summoning the spirits of the dead since as early as the ancient Greeks. For this purpose it was burned on a fire of privet, the wood chosen for use in funeral pyres, as it was felt that a fire of privet opened the doors to the underworld. In Christian practice it is said that wormwood was cast out of the garden of Eden with Adam and

Eve. One might say that wormwood has a rather unsavory reputation.

To use wormwood to summon the spirits of the dead, it should be finely ground and burned on charcoal as an incense. Wormwood can be used either to summon a spirit into a medium, or to summon a spirit into visible appearance. It is not as effective as Solomon's seal root for spiritual forces or non-human entities, but it is excellent when working with the dead of the human community.

Wormwood can also be used in making love charms and for other work requiring a change in the astral condition. The use of wormwood in summoning spirits is its most important use in magic, however. In working with the dead, it finds a place filled by no other herb.

Those who would like to work with the dead may use the following incenses for summoning. There is a great deal more to working with the dead than having the proper incense at hand, but use of a good incense will certainly assist matters.

Summoning incense number one:

3 parts wormwood herb
1 part Solomon's seal herb

This incense is useful for summoning recalcitrant spirits— those who are not in the best mood when they are summoned. It must not be used when attempting to summon higher spirits, but it is excellent for summoning the human dead.

Summoning incense number two:

3 parts wormwood herb
1 part vervain herb

This incense is useful for summoning people who died in a depressed state, or people who are not aware they are dead. It is useful for lightening up spirits who are sad, as well as calling them to you. It will generally call a more elevated type of spirit than the first incense, but its action is much the same.

YARROW

Yarrow is probably best known for its use in casting the *I Ching*. The small fresh leaves of yarrow which are plucked during the time immediately following the new moon in Taurus are also one of the most potent materials available for increasing love. Thus Yarrow forms the ideal love charm material.

Yarrow picked at any other time will promote the growth of love as well. A tea made with a tablespoon of yarrow over which a cup of boiling water has been poured may be used in a bath, floorwash, or as a sprinkle to increase the capacity for love in the place where it is used. In a bath it will assist one to locate a lover.

7 Spells of Obeah & Wanga

Obeah and Wanga are the names of two religio-magical practices of African origin that are found primarily in the British colonies of the New World. They have lost much of their African background, and most of its religious associations. What remains is the magical practice. The names of the former religious practices now simply mean a spell. Ju-ju is another word with a similar meaning.

The spell indicated by any of these words may be used for either good or evil purposes. Since good spells are seldom complained about, the phrase usually heard is on the order of, "He put a wanga on me!" Occasionally one is asked for a specific wanga, but usually money or love charms are desired, with the spell being left up to the person making it.

Spells of obeah and wanga usually involve a magical charm of one sort of another. The charm may be made from natural ingredients, such as herbs, or the charm may be a manufactured item, such as an amulet. Obeah and wanga spells are rarely spoken charms; they are, or result in, real physical things. A material object is involved in the work. If the spell is a curse, the discovery and subsequent destruction of the material object will void the curse.

At the present time in the United States, the most common of these charms are the charm bags worn or carried for some particular purpose. They are often worn around the neck of those who believe in them. For the most part these are protective spells or charms. They are intended to keep negative energy away from the wearer, or add some quality which is desired. Negative wangas are usually placed near the home or workplace of the person they are designed to affect.

A sampling of these wangas follows, although any of the spells in this book which result in a physical object will serve as a wanga. Wangas are infinite in variety, both in kind and in purpose. The first wanga preparation I witnessed resulted in a liquid, which was to be poured on the steps of someone's house. The liquid contained a number of ingredients, and it was not as simple as the spells in this book.

The charm bags which ordinarily contain the herbs and material used to make obeah and wanga are sewn from ordinary cloth, although purists prefer cotton flannel. A piece of cloth about three by five inches is cut and folded in half. It is then sewn on two sides, and the material put into the bag. The remaining side is then sewn shut. In occult stores it is possible to purchase bags which are made for this purpose. These bags have a string closure which allows them to be used by those who do not sew.

Those who practice ceremonial magic according to the *Book of the Law* transmitted to Aleister Crowley will find a reference there to obeah and wanga.[1] These spells might be of interest on that account and are much simpler than most ceremonial magic.

---

[1]Crowley, *Book of the Law* (York Beach, ME: Samuel Weiser, 1976), p. 23.

NUTMEG SPELL

Nutmeg is often used as a charm. In addition to relating astrologically to Jupiter, it has the reputation of bringing money to the person who carries it. Nutmeg has been used as a charm because at one time having nutmeg in the house was a display of prosperity. Nutmeg strengthens the Jupiterian influence around you if you carry it.

A typical charm or wanga made from the nutmeg is called "the gambler's nutmeg." The charm is so popular in certain areas of the country that at one time it had an unofficial "fair trade" price of $25.00 in New York City. The popularity of the charm attests to its effectiveness. It is carried by people who gamble, by businesspeople, and by those who simply are asking for assistance in their economic evolution.

The nutmeg charm is usually supplied in a chamois skin or red flannel charm bag. The person who supplies the charm will usually instruct the purchaser in the following rules for its use. First, your wanga should be carried on your person. At night it should be kept with your personal belongings in the bedroom. During the day it may either be carried in purse, pocket, or worn around the neck in a charm bag.

Second, the wanga should be discarded if it drops to the floor or is broken in any way. In this event, you should return to the person who prepared the charm to find out if a new wanga is needed. It frequently happens that the first charm is lost in this way, usually after a few days or a week. This is not really a loss, as the charm has filled its function. It is usually an indication that you should replace the charm, as the influences which blocked the accomplishment of the work of the charm have now been removed.

Third, the charm should be treated with respect. It is a living thing, and if you own it, you are asking it to work for you – to do what you cannot. By respecting the charm, you are demonstrating that you will allow it to work for you. This means that you will not show it to others, or treat the charm in a negative manner, such as tossing it around or thinking badly of it. These are the basic rules of a wanga. Some people who prepare charms will add more rules as to how to treat them, and with some charms, this advice is vital.

To make your own "Gambler's Nutmeg," take a whole nutmeg, and drill a small hole in the stem end, about half way into the nutmeg. Clean out the shavings and put a drop of mercury into the hole. Seal the hole closed with a few drops of red sealing wax. Anoint the circumference of the nutmeg with a dab of sandalwood oil, and pray over it for yourself or for the person you are making it for. Place the nutmeg in a new charm pouch and it is ready to use.

This is a fairly simple wanga, and you will have an opportunity to test yourself when you make it. If you have been having money problems, they should begin to clear up in a month or so. The number of people who use this charm should convince the most hardened skeptic of its benefit. It has a positive effect on most people, and is certainly worth trying.

LUCKY HAND SPELL

The Lucky Hand spell is another standard wanga. It is a specific type of charm bag, made to "give a hand" to the person using it. It has the effect of making your life a bit easier by bringing you good fortune and opportunity. This particular spell comes from the North Carolina Gulta practice.

Three herbs must be gathered and prepared for the charm. First is a sand burr, the seed of the sand nettle. Second is a piece of Sampson snakeroot, which must be broken off, not cut with a knife. Third is a piece of devil's shoestrings, or goat's rue. These three herbs are wrapped in a small piece of black cloth, which is then sewn closed all around with white thread. The stitches in the packet should be as small as possible.

The packet is set to soak in a small glass of whiskey, either all day or overnight. It is then taken out and prayed over. The whiskey is left to evaporate in the glass. The finished charm is placed in a charm bag or a leather bag. It can be talked to for any specific request which you want to make of it. This charm brings opportunities; it will not do the work required to bring them to fruition.

LOVE SPELL

This is a rather well-known love spell. It is popular, and it works. If you use this spell, remove the red charm bag before having sex, but hide it.

Take two sewing needles of the same size, and lay them side by side, with the point of one at the eye of the other. Wrap the two needles in the leaf of a comfrey plant, or any other green leaf that has been newly picked. Tie this bundle with a piece of red wool yarn. Place the finished packet in either a red fabric or a chamois skin bag. It is then worn around your neck to gain the affection of the one you desire.

The charm may be removed from the bag only to break it, which is done by breaking the two needles. If it is desired to "feed" the charm for a specific person, it should be fed through the opened bag with three drops of whiskey. It can be prayed over at this time to tell it who it is you wish to influence.

BLESSED HANDKERCHIEF SPELL

This spell actually forms a part of protestant Christian magical practice, and takes its authority from the Bible. It is used in some protestant churches as a means of extending the power of the minister or the pastor of the church to those members of the congregation who may not be able to attend regular services, or who may be located far from the church. There is a real purpose to this type of spell or "talisman": if it is properly prepared it has the effect of connecting the person who has the completed handkerchief with the spiritual force of the pastor or minister who prepared it.

It is easy to look at the preparation of these artifacts as a superstition and to say that they are of little or no real value.

However, there are many cases of people who were healed of various afflictions through the use of one of these prepared handkerchiefs. At worst, they are a comfort to those who possess them and believe in their beneficial effect. Our materialistic age is too quick to condemn as superstition anything that does not fit into the scheme of academic science. If we were able to understand the realities of the non-physical world, we might see that there is a great deal more to some "superstitions" than science is willing to accept! It would be better to postpone judgment until we know the truth of such things.

The Biblical authority for this spell comes from the Book of Acts in the New Testament. Chapter 19 Verses 11–12 (King James translation) state:

11 – And God wrought special miracles by the hands of Paul:
12 – So that from his body were brought unto the sick handkerchiefs or aprons, and the diseases departed from them, and the evil spirits went out of them.

According to Christian tradition, Saint Paul was granted a mission by Christ to carry the word of Christ to the gentiles. It is assumed that he also was granted the spiritual force to accomplish this mission, and that his spiritual force, penetrating his garments, is what made them a connection to him, and thus able to heal the sick and the insane. The preparation of a blessed prayer handkerchief is then simply a matter of imbuing the handkerchief with as much spiritual force as the minister or pastor can.

Since these handkerchiefs are usually made in quantity for distribution, it is frequently difficult for a minister or a pastor to "charge them" effectively. In some cases they are simply placed on the altar and prayed over. The following procedure will provide a fairly uniform charge to about a dozen handkerchiefs at a time, without violating any of the magical taboos of most of the protestant sects that use these handkerchiefs.

First the handkerchiefs are opened (i.e., not folded) and placed in a stack on the altar. Then holy water is prepared in whatever way the particular denomination of the religion calls for. Consecrated salt, usually a part of the preparation of holy water, is prepared in excess, and set aside as well. The holy water and the salt are placed on the altar. Incense of whatever kind the denomination prescribes is also prepared, and set on the altar. If no incense is specified, High Spirit Incense is recommended, as found on page 53 of this book.

After making an invocation at the altar, the minister blesses all of the handkerchiefs. He then takes them, one at a time, and fumigates them individually in the incense, sprinkles them with holy water and sets them aside on the altar. Any customary prayers of blessing can be used, or the minister can devise a set form for these prayers if he wishes. Then, all the handkerchiefs are folded at the altar with a bit (a few grains) of the consecrated salt inside each of them. If they are to be blessed individually in the names of the congregation members, it is worthwhile to have namecards placed alongside the handkerchiefs so that the blessing can be made individually and the handkerchief identified from that point on.

Once all the handkerchiefs have been blessed, the service is closed with a simple benediction. The finished handkerchiefs are now ready to be distributed. If they are not distributed immediately, they should be placed in individual envelopes so they will be kept out of contact from any other influence while they are in storage.

These handkerchiefs are also made by counselors for distribution to clients, but they are rarely used by those who are practitioners of magic. They do make an effective gift to a troubled client, and probably should be more widely used.

8 *Spoken Spells*

The Pennsylvania Dutch Hexenmeisters work almost entirely with spoken spells. Many other practices use spoken spells, and differentiate them from the use of prayers. In fact a spoken spell is a prayer, but it is not a prayer in accordance with the suggestions for prayer made by Christ as recorded in the Gospel of Matthew 6:6. The spoken spell is said before the person for whom the work is being done, and the force of the spell itself is what causes the work to be accomplished.

That the spoken word has real force is beyond question. Yet the power of the spoken word is not usually realized in our present society. One of the great Indian spiritual teachers of this century had the following to say about the power of the spoken word:

A man's words are lifeless if he fails to impregnate them with spiritual force. Talkativeness, exaggeration or falsehood makes your words as ineffective as paper bullets shot from a toy gun. The speech of garrulous or inaccurate persons are unlikely to produce any beneficial changes in the order of things. Man's words should represent not only truth but also his definite understanding and realization. Speech without soul force is like husks without corn.[1]

To be operative, the spoken spell must contain the full faith and belief of the person speaking it. It must also project into the person, place, or thing to which it is spoken. This is the reason for the voice exercises that are given to students of magic. Voice technique must be mastered before this kind of spell is fully operative. When one speaks the spell, he or she is actually affecting matter with the voice, and actually transforms it in accord with the will.

The manner in which this kind of spell is spoken is of primary importance. It must be spoken with absolute conviction, and in an emotional and energetic manner. This is not a manner of speech which is easily learned, but it can be learned and *must* be mastered by those who would learn these spells. The speaker's voice must resonate conviction so strongly that the words pass out and surround the person and area they are spoken for with a real and living spiritual force. Many of these spells were given to me by practitioners who regularly use them.

A number of spells in this section come from the Christian religious practice. Most of these are not recognized by the established Christian Church today. They are still used by those who believe in them, however, and they work in the proper hands. The sincere prayer of anyone who believes is heard, regardless of the theological position at the time. Theology changes, God does not.

---

[1]Yogananda, *Scientific Healing Affirmations* (Los Angeles: Self Realization Fellowship, 1981), p. 15.

TO STOP BLOOD

The first spell that every hex healer learns is the spell to stop blood. If you cannot use this spell to aid people who have cut themselves, it is unlikely that you will be able to make much progress in learning to heal other infirmities. The ability to stop blood is basic to the healer's art, and any person who would be a healer must first begin with this or one similar. This spell is in daily use by many hex healers in Pennsylvania, and it works according to the ability of the healer.

> Jesus Christ, dearest blood!
> That stoppeth the pain and stoppeth the blood.
> In this help you *(first name),* God the Father,
> God the Son, God the Holy Ghost. Amen.[2]

The spell is to be repeated over the person's wound, or facing the direction in which the injured person is. Then three signs of the cross are made over the wound, or in the same direction, one after another. The spell should be repeated again in half an hour, in the same way.

TO STOP FIRE

Fire is a rural disaster. It brings total economic ruin to a farm family. There are a number of charms against the spread of fire. They work according to the ability of the person using them. The following charm is to be spoken at the fire itself to halt its spread.

> Our dear Sarah journeyed through the land,
> having a fiery hot brand in her hand.
> The fiery brand heats; the fiery brand sweats.

[2]John Hohman, *Pow-Wows or the Long Lost Friend* (Brooklyn, NY: Fulton Religious Supply Co., 1820), p. 17.

Fiery brand, stop your heat:
Fiery brand, stop your sweat.[3]

A SPELL FOR SWELLINGS

This spell comes from a work which is quite popular among Hexers called *Alburtus Magnus,* or the *Egyptian Secrets.*[4] The book is popular in Germany, and widely sold in the United States. It was not written by Alburtus Magnus, but it is attributed to him because of his widespread reputation as a magician and wizard.

Swelling, swelling, swelling,
In the name of Jesus, I command thee,
That thou shalt cause _____,
As little pain as the three nails caused
Our Saviour Jesus Christ.

Make three signs of the cross over the swelling. Repeat the spell in a half hour, as above.

TO EXORCISE AN EVIL SPIRIT

The person making the prayer of exorcism faces the one afflicted and repeats the following, saying it three times, aloud and in a clear voice.

Thou arch-sorcerer, thou has attacked _____;
let that witchcraft receed from him into thy marrow
and into thy bone, let it be returned unto thee. I exorcise thee for the five wounds of Jesus, thou evil spirit,
and conjure thee for the five wounds of Jesus of this

[3]*Pow-Wows or the Long Lost Friend*, p. 53.
[4]*The Book of Secrets of Alburtus Magnus* (NY: Oxford University Press, 1973).

flesh, marrow and bone; I exorcise thee for the sake of
the five wounds of Jesus, at this very hour restore to
health again _____, in the name of God
the Father, God the Son, and God the Holy Spirit.

Three signs of the cross should be made at the end of each
prayer.

TO STOP THE PAIN OF A FRESH WOUND

Say the following to the person in a clear voice, making the
signs of the cross over the wound where indicated at the end of
the prayer.

> Our beloved Lord Jesus Christ had many boils and
> wounds, but never had them bound. They do not
> become sore, they fester not, neither do they suppu-
> rate. Jonas was blind, when I, the heavenly child said
> unto him: As true as the holy five wounds were
> inflicted, and did not curdle nor fester. From them I
> take water and blood, that is for all hurts and injuries
> good. Holy is the man who can heal all wounds and
> injuries. Amen.

TO PREVENT A BURN FROM
CAUSING PAIN

The following spell should be recited softly but firmly by the
person who is working the spell, while holding his or her hand
over the burned area. If the burn is extensive, the hand should
be moved to a different part of the burned area and the spell
repeated until the entire area of the burn is covered. This is a
famous charm for removing the pain from a burn, and has been
used with excellent results for many years. I was unable to
write about it until I recently found it in print, as it had been
given to me in secret many years ago.

Fire of God,
Lose thy heat,
As Judas lost his color
When he betrayed our Lord
In the Garden of Olives.[5]

NIGHTLY PROTECTION OF THE HOME

When preparing for bed, you may protect your home through
the use of the following prayer. Kneel at your bedside and say
the following prayer four times.

My Home has four corners
Four Holy Angels adorn them,
Matthew, Mark, Luke and John.

Neither Witches, nor Charmers,
Nor those who do evil
May harm me or mine.

My home has four corners
Four Holy Angels adorn them
Matthew, Mark, Luke and John.

My home stands with Christ,
Surrounded by the Angels,
Protected from evil
Which would harm me or mine.

In the name of the Father,
And of the Son,
And of the Holy Spirit,
Amen.[6]

---

[5]Papus, *What Is Occultism?* (Albuquerque, NM: Sun Books, 1981), p. 69.
[6]This spell was given to me as a gift from a Blue Ball, PA, Hexenmeister in
1980.

TO RELIEVE MALOCHIA

Malochia, or the Evil Eye, is a physical condition with an entirely psychic cause. It is found as an otherwise unexplanable headache or a sudden backache with no known origin. The following is one of a number of spells which may be used to relieve the condition. It is notable in that it is one of the few spells which you can use to cure malochia for yourself. It may be repeated every half hour for three repetitions for complete relief from a severe attack.

Place a teaspoon of olive oil in a small dish. Pray the following prayer over it.

Adoni, Lord of the worlds, visible and invisible, be my physician and comfort me in my distress. Heal and remove from me this which has been placed on me to aggrieve my head and my back. Thou art my only help, Thou art my only counsel, Thou art my only source of action. Come to my help I pray thee to give me healing. Amen.[7]

Anoint your temples, the top of your head and the bump at the back of your head with the oil.

PRAYER BEFORE WORKING

This is a prayer to be said on a daily basis. It is a spoken spell and is used with the intent of overcoming all obstacles to the work at hand. The prayer is also used by a few Hexenmeisters as they prepare to do healings or to make charms.

Jesus Christ, Saviour of Man,
I ask that you aid me in my work.
Almighty God, Creator of Man,
I ask that you aid me in my work.
Holy Spirit, Witness and Guide,
I ask that you aid me in my work.

[7]This spell was a gift from an Ephrata, PA, Hexenmeister, 1979.

Beloved Holy Trinity, mighty and mysterious, I ask that through the intercession of the angels my work prosper on this day, and that I be kept from all bad things. I shall be bound to the right, the good and the proper, and I shall see the work before me through the eyes of God, so that I may be led safely through all temptation to the profit of my immortal soul.

God be with me on this day.

Christ be with me on this day.

Holy Spirit be with me on this day.

I ask this in the name of Almighty God whose ears are never deaf to any appeal, who helps repentant sinners such as I to reach the glory of eternity through his mercy and his love.

Amen.

This prayer may be used as a daily prayer being regularly spoken before leaving the house to go to work. Used in this way, it shows the one who prays it the true relationship between self, work and creator. Over time it will allow the one who uses it to grow closer in daily life to the will of God.

CONTRACTING THROUGH TAKING AN OATH

The process of taking an oath is held with awe and reverence in most primitive societies. In our modern and supposedly enlightened society, it is not held in such high esteem. Among some of the rural Hexenmeisters on the eastern seaboard, the taking of a serious oath is held in a different light from taking a civil oath. Agreeing to purchase a farm, to enter into a business, or to care for a friend's children after his or her death is a very serious step, and it requires a serious oath.

The following form of oath taking is considered to be a "serious oath," and it is thought that one who breaks such an oath loses all chances of divine salvation or eternal grace. Oaths which are sworn in this way are usually held to be beyond breaking, and should they be broken, the individual is treated by his former friends and neighbors as if he were eternally damned. This is a much more severe form of shunning, in that the oath breaker is not even recognized, much less spoken to. He is usually unable to conduct any business at all, and certainly cannot borrow money from anyone in his community.

The process of taking the oath is as follows: Both parties read the oath with their hands on a copy of the Bible. When the prayer is finished, the two parties shake hands and the oath is complete. The agreement is usually written out in full, and read by the parties agreeing to the various parts. In most cases there are two or three witnesses for each party present. The added social pressure of the oath takers knowing that the witnesses will inform the community at large makes the breaking of the oath a very unlikely act. In some cases the oath is taken after a regular Sunday church service.

> I swear by God the Father Almighty, and by Jesus Christ, his only begotten Son, and by the Holy Spirit, ever present and all knowing, that I enter into the following agreement with _____ of my own free will and desire, and that I shall keep it as a cornerstone of my life or forfeit such grace toward salvation as my soul shall earn.
>
> I agree that _____ .
>
> All this do I swear with my right hand on God's holy word, calling upon God the Father, Jesus Christ his Son, and the Holy Spirit to bear witness to this and knowing that all of the angels of heaven will now aid me in keeping to my oath and contract, or they will punish me eternally should I break it. Amen.

PRAYER TO SAINT HELEN FOR
SIGHT IN THE CRYSTAL

I found the following prayer in an old booklet dating back to
the 1860's which describes the manner of making a crystal,
consecrating and using it. The consecration involves it being
blessed during the saying of a mass, so it would be difficult to
suppose it could be done by anyone who was not a Roman
Catholic priest. The booklet is attributed to (St.) Thomas the
Ox of Christ, better known as the Dominican theologian St.
Thomas Aquinas. It is unlikely, however, that he was the real
author.

The prayer given below is to be said over the crystal before
looking into it. It is to be spoken aloud as would befit a prayer
made for the person who is to look into the crystal for another.
The text did not specify whether this was quartz crystal or
lead crystal – you will probably want to use quartz.

I pray thee, Holy Lady Helen, mother of King Constantine, who didst discover the cross of our Lord
Jesus Christ, by that most sacred devotion and find-
ing of the Holy Cross, and by that Most Holy Cross,
and by the joy which thou hadst when thou didst find
that Most Holy Cross, and by the love which thou
hadst for thy son King Constantine, and by all the
blessings which thou enjoyest perpetually, that thou
should show me in this crystal whatever I seek and
desire to know. Amen.

ISLAMIC PRAYERS AGAINST EVIL

Moslem religious practice has a rich and varied source of magi-
cal spells and charms in the form of the Surah's of the Koran.
This book, revealed entirely through the agency of the prophet
Mohammed, is the Holy Book and the foundation of Islam.
The last two Surah's of the Koran were revealed especially for
the protection of humankind against evil.

The Koran, because of its peculiar nature in the tongue in which it was written, cannot be even approximately translated into another language. The last two Surahs are included here for the use for which they were originally intended.

SURAH CXIII

The Daybreak

In the name of Allah, the Beneficent, the Merciful,
Say: I seek refuge in the Lord of the Daybreak
From the evil of that which he created;
From the evil of the darkness when it is intense,
And from the evil of malignant witchcraft,
And from the evil of the envier when he envieth.

SURAH CXIV

Mankind

In the name of Allah, the Beneficent, the Merciful.
Say: I seek refuge in the Lord of Mankind,
The King of Mankind,
The God of Mankind,
From the evil of the sneaking whisperer,
Who whispereth in the hearts of mankind,
Of the jinn and of mankind.[8]

THE PRAYER OF THE
SEVEN AFRICAN TOOLS

This prayer is a combination of the Yoruba Nigerian pantheon in African magico-religious practice, and the Christian pantheon of Christ, the apostles and the saints. The two mythologies are blended in the traditional belief that Christ was a

---

[8]This translation is from *The Meaning of the Glorious Koran* by Mohammed Marmaduke Pickthall (NY: New American Library, Mentor Books, 1978), p. 455.

carpenter, and that the seven principal deities of the Yoruba pantheon use tools to do their work on the earth. It is a spoken spell, in that it works to effect changes in the life of the person who prays it with sincerity over a period of time.

The seven deities of the Yoruba pantheon are:

Chango (Sh-ang-go): The deity of fire, male virility, benevolence and wealth. He is similar to the Roman deity Jupiter.

Orula (Oh-rule-ah): The deity of fate who sends humankind to earth with a life to live and a destiny to work out.

Ogun (Oh-goon): The deity of iron, craftsmanship, surgery, manual skills and warfare. He is similar to the Roman deity Mars.

Elegua (E-leg-wa): The deity of the crossroads and trickster of the Yoruba pantheon. He is similar to the Roman Mercury.

Obatala (Oh-baa-ta-la): The deity of morality, spiritual growth, purity and kingship.

Yemaya (Yem-ah-yah): The Mother Goddess of the Yoruba pantheon, she is the "owner of the sea," and deity of salt water.

Oschun (Oh-shoe-n): She is the deity of gracious living and entertainment. Similar to the Roman Venus.

The seven tools mentioned in the following prayer are gathered together. Beginning on any convenient day, the prayer is made holding each of the tools in your hand in turn, and setting each tool down to pick up the next one at the next line of the prayer. At the end of the prayer of the tools, they are put away saying, "In the Name of the Father, the Son and the Holy Ghost, that they grant my wish for what I need most."

The prayer must be prayed with fervor and sincerity for seven consecutive days, to begin to effect changes in your life. At the end of the first week, conditions usually begin to change, and after the second week of continuous prayer, the most needful condition is in the process of being remedied.

I pray that the Seven Powers come to my aid.

Chango, you are the hammer, and I pray to you that
    I may have fulfillment in love.

Orula, you are the saw, and I pray to you that all
   obstacles may be removed from my life.

Ogun, you are the chisel, and I pray to you that you
   make my dreams come true.

Elegua, you are the mallet, and I pray to you that
   you make me dominate over my enemies.

Obatala, you are the wrench, and I pray to you that
   I have money for my needs.

Yemaya, you are the pliers, and I pray to you that I
   gain power and success.

Oschun, you are the hatchet, and I pray to you to
   protect me against all evil.

I pray that the seven powers come to my aid in the
name of the Father and the Son and the Holy Ghost,
and that they grant my wish for what I need most.

9 *Written Spells*

Spoken spells have a transitory force, affecting only the action to which they are directed. Written spells, on the other hand, are thought to last as long as the written spell is in existence. To maintain the long term effect of the written spell, many of the prayers of the Egyptians were written on coffins and placed in the *Book of the Dead* with the mummy.

As written spells combine the effect of symbols, these spells are thought to be far more potent than any other kind. The Islamic Koran is, as the revealed word of God, a sort of written spell in itself. Anyone who has heard it read aloud in Arabic knows that it is also a spoken spell of great beauty, even to those who cannot understand the language. The Latin psalms have the same quality, but without the tonal beauty which is found in the Arabic language.

Older written spells on parchment, some of which have been in existence for hundreds of years, are particularly revered. In many cases their real effect lies in the fact that so many people believe in them. Some older writings have taken on a "magical aura" solely due to their age.

Because of their strangeness and the mystical power associated with strangeness, spells written in a foreign language or in a mystical or "magical" alphabet are also thought to have great power. This is one reason why spells written in Hebrew characters are supposed to be superior in quality. In the Middle Ages, a talisman was a man who wore a tallis, the shirt or undershirt worn by orthodox Jews. As this was felt to be a source of power to them, the idea of "talisman" quickly transfered to a spell written to give power or protection. In the first thousand years of Christianity, Hebrew was the pre-eminent language for the writing of spells, and Jews, who were the most literate members of any European community, were the pre-eminent "magicians of choice."

This obviously lead to some silly situations. One old "authentic spell" in a European museum was removed from display when it was pointed out that the words of the spell said, "What is the meaning of this?" in Hebrew characters transliterating medieval French! It had been supposed to be a spell to call upon a demon to cure sick children.

Written spells form another branch of the spell-caster's art. In the Hex practice of the Pennsylvania Dutch country, himmelbriefs, or "heavenly letters," are designed to act to protect the one who carries them against ills and evils of all kinds. The older versions were written with painstaking care by the hexenmeister who copied them one letter at a time. The newer versions are usually mimeographed copies of a typed original which are sold for a dollar or two as curios.

Just as a spoken spell requires a certain ability to use one's voice, a written spell requires a certain ability to concentrate upon what one is writing, and hold the image of the desired work for the spell throughout the entire operation. The spell should be written with a new pen, or at least a pen which is used only for writing spells. It must be written with absolute concentration on every letter of the spell. It should then be read aloud in the same manner when it is finished. If the spell is to be given to someone it should be enclosed in an envelope, but not sealed. Most of these spells are to be carried on the person when they are in use.

The first spell in this section is an example of a symbol and a spoken spell or prayer. The other written spells are well-known gnostic spells or modern hex spells.

STAR OF DAVID SPELL

The Star of David, two interlaced equilateral triangles, has a great history as a magical amulet. Not only is it the symbol of the Jewish religion and the Hebrew people, it is also an occult symbol of continuing repute. It is not a symbol in the sense of the Ve-Ves of the Vodun religious-magico practice. It is a particular occult statement of fact which must be experienced to be understood. It is still used as a symbol of power by those who believe in it.

The Star of David is used to grant wishes by inscribing it on a piece of paper. The symbol is held at arm's length and the individual's wish is spoken aloud three times. It is then felt that the wish will come true. See figure 2.

Figure 2.   The Star of David.

```
S A T O R
A R E P O
T E N E T
O P E R A
R O T A S
```

Figure 3.   The Sator Spell.

SATOR SPELL

The Sator Spell is one of the oldest written spells known to humans. It has been found wherever the Roman legions marched – from England to Egypt. At one time, in parts of medieval Germany it was required that every house have a plaque which had the Sator Spell written on it. The plaque was to be thrown into any house that was on fire to aid in putting out the fire! I guess you could call it an occult fire extinguisher.

The spell has also been used as a love spell, and for any number of other purposes. Its origin is in doubt, and learned scholars debate its meaning. The only thing that we know for certain about it is that it is both old and well known.

For use as a protection against fire in a house the spell is written on a piece of paper or parchment and placed at the highest point of the house, inside the house. See figure 3.

ABRACADABRA SPELL

This is one of the most widespread spells of all time. Supposedly taking its origins from the gnostic Christians of about 300 A.D., it is now thought to date from a much earlier time. It is written as a spell against fever, which is supposed to disappear just as the name Abracadabra disappears from the spell.

A B R A C A D A B R A

A B R A C A D A B R

A B R A C A D A B

A B R A C A D A

A B R A C A D

A B R A C A

A B R A C

A B R A

A B R

A B

A

Figure 4. The Abracadabra Spell.

The charm is to be written out and hung around the neck of the person to be healed. Its longevity seems to testify to its ability to heal. See figure 4.

BANISHING SPELL

The spell shown in Figure 5 was written on parchment or paper to cause negative forces to leave the place where it was displayed. It was said to be so powerful that it would drive away the devil himself. It uses the name of a gnostic deity form, but like most spells of this type it is probably not the same as the original gnostic use of the charm.

ABRAXAS
BRAXAS
RAXAS
AXAS
XAS
AS
S

Figure 5. The Abraxas Spell.

A SPELL FOR SAFETY FROM GYPSIES

Apparently the author of *Alburtus Magnus* felt that the Gypsies were able to outsmart him easily. He included the following spell in his book of *Egyptian Secrets,* to be carried to protect people against "the arts and wiles of Gypsies."

> Just the same as the prophet Jonah, the prototype of Christ, had been provided for during three days and three nights in the body of the whale, so may Almighty God protect me against all danger with his fatherly kindness.

WATER SPELL

This is a more advanced kind of written spell. A spell usually for protection or healing, is written on parchment paper with a water-soluble ink. The spell is then prayed over in the usual way and the ink is washed off the paper into water. The water is then used as the medium of the spell. The person for whom the spell is made can wash in the water, or the water may be used for washing floors, etc. In some cases, the water is sprinkled over an area where the person is to walk.

Rice paper, which dissolves in water, may also be used to write the spell on. The written spell, as it dissolves into the water, can make quite an impression on the mind of the person who has never seen this happen before! This is particularly true if spirit seals also form a part of the spell.

10 *Miscellaneous Spells*

There is no end to the number and kinds of spells you can learn to cast. This present work has been a guide to get you started. This chapter includes a miscellany that may interest you. The spells listed here fall into no real category, yet they have been used successfully for many years by the practitioners who taught them to me.

SEVEN KNOB WISHING CANDLE SPELL

This is a means of fulfilling a wish which you know is possible to bring to fulfillment. Wishes that are not possible are usually not worth going after. It is important to know what you want and go after it. If you have a clear idea of what you want, and if it is something that it is possible for you to have, you can usually get it.

First purchase a seven knob wishing candle at an occult or curio store. This is a candle with seven distinct knobs on it, usually all of one color.

Second, write out your wish, simply as possible, using as few words as possible. The candle should be rubbed with a bit of cooking oil to which you have added a drop of your favorite perfume.

When the Moon is new, place the candle on the paper with the wish, light it, and let the first knob burn down while you concentrate on your desire. This is continued for seven days, burning one knob each day while concentrating on your desire, your wish.

For the next seven days the burned-out candle is left on the paper on which the wish is written. At the end of the week, the wish is usually on the way to fulfillment and the candle remains and the paper may be discarded.

FOUR THIEVES VINEGAR

Four Thieves Vinegar is one of the tastiest salad dressings you'll ever experience. It also has a wide-ranging reputation for healing and practical magic. For healing, it is used as a preventative tonic against all sorts of diseases, although its reputation was gained as a preventative against the bubonic plague in the Middle Ages. It is also used as a wound dressing in the old style treatment of gangrene, being applied to the wound after the maggotts have eaten off the dead flesh. It is not recommended for healing anymore, as there are more conventional ways of treating these illnesses.

To make the original Four Thieves Vinegar, peel a number of cloves of garlic. Place the garlic in a clean glass bottle. When the bottle is full of peeled garlic cloves, wine vinegar is poured over the garlic until the bottle is full. The bottle can then be capped and placed in the refrigerator, root cellar, or spring house for a week or so. The vinegar should be used a little at a time, with new wine vinegar being added as some is drawn out. It will last a year or so before a new batch needs to be made.

Purists use a red Bordeaux wine, and wait for it to turn to vinegar before using it. With modern pasteurized wines this may take some time, so wine vinegar is a faster starting place. Apple cider vinegar is not the "real thing" but it works just as well in magic and better for some healing work.

Four Thieves Vinegar Tonic

This is a spring tonic which is also good for occasional use in the heat of the summer. It adds potassium to the system, and is supposed to clean the blood. It is definitely a home remedy curio – and is not included here as a serious medical recommendation.

Take a tablespoon of Four Thieves Vinegar, place it in a small glass or cup. Add a teaspoon of honey and mix. Then add a tablespoon of hot water and drink it.

Four Thieves Vinegar Spell

This spell is used to keep a person from drinking. Mix one of his or her favorite drinks, and place some of it in a small bottle which has a secure cap. Add the same amount of Four Thieves Vinegar to the bottle while you pray that his or her drink will turn sour in the mouth, and sit uneasily on the stomach. Then cap the bottle and seal it with tape – cellophane tape will do fine.

Lastly, pray that the person – call him or her by name – will be unable to drink the drink so long as the bottle remains sealed. This spell is one that is used quite often, but it has a remarkable disadvantage. If the person is a committed drunk you will now have to find out what his or her new favorite drink is!

Four Thieves Vinegar Rub

Combine one-fourth cup of Four Thieves Vinegar and three-fourths cup water. Using a wash cloth, wash yourself down from head to toe after a cool shower. This is a particularly good rubdown for the first shower after a debilitating illness. You may wish to shower again after the rubdown, however. It assists in removing dead skin and negative vibrations, so it has both a cosmetic and an astral cleansing effect.

Move Out Of My Life Spell

Place the name of the person you wish out of your life in a small bottle. Fill the bottle full with Four Thieves Vinegar and cap it securely. Throw the bottle into a river while praying that the person will leave your life.

LODESTONE SPELLS

Lodestones are natural magnets. For many years they have been used in all sorts of spells, primarily to attract things to the one using them. We met them first under Magnet Oil in the section on oils. Because lodestones move without being touched, they seem to be the best example of living beings in the mineral world.

They have been used in magic by a number of cultures. As a result they have accumulated a wide range of spells around them. Most of these spells are based on the property of the lodestone to attract small bits of iron. Many modern magicians prefer the more powerful alnico or ceramic magnets available today. Any of these may be used to good effect for the following spells.

Lodestone Good Luck Charm

Keep a lodestone in a covered earthenware dish. Once a week, on the same day, take it out of the dish and place it in a glass of water. Let it sit in the water for a few minutes while you thank it for its help in attracting good things into your life in the last week. Then take the lodestone out of the water and drink the water. Dry the lodestone and place it back in its container, sprinkling a few pinches of "magnetic sand" (iron filings) over it, and put it away in its container until the next week.

You must keep the lodestone out of sight, usually in a closet or other private place. You can tell the lodestone just what you want by "programing it" with symbols. For example, to gain increased income, place a silver dime in the container with it. For love, you could put a photo of someone in the container. The purpose of the lodestone is to assist you in drawing to you those things you want to have in life.

Lodestone Healing Spell

I must admit that I have only met one person who could use this spell successfully. She was an old woman who did root working in the Sweetwater, Tennessee, area in the late 1930's and early 1940's. I will tell you the procedure she used, and hope that you also can do it.

Pray over a lodestone, which is kept in a red charm bag and used only for healing. Tell the lodestone you want it to remove all sickness from the person, naming the person by name. Then take the lodestone and pass it over the person's body from head to foot, one stroke at a time. After each stroke the stone is to be dipped in a bucket of cool water. This requires about fifty strokes, from the center of the head to the toes and then to the bucket of water. If the person is bed-ridden, he or she is turned over to allow the magnet to stroke every part of the body. Once the stroking is completed, the lodestone is thanked and replaced in the bag. The bucket of water is emptied in the middle of a road. Be careful that it does not splash on the person who empties it.

Lodestone Charms

Lodestone charms are occasionally made into charm bags. In this case they are usually "fed" with iron on a regular basis. In addition, the charms are usually made up with herbs or some form of symbol to indicate just what is to be drawn to the wearer. I know a young man who had one made up with a tiny automobile to assist him in obtaining a car. He was able to buy the car he wanted after wearing the charm for a month or so.

BATH SALTS

Bath salts are often used for protective or healing baths. They are easy to make, and you can save a lot of money by making your own rather than buying the prepared product at an occult or curio store. The end result is a bathing product which may have a spiritual effect, which is to say that the bath salt might cleanse away some astral detritus when you use it. However, it doesn't work for everyone. If you don't like swimming in the ocean you should not use this type of bath.

Take a cup of rock salt, such as the sodium chloride used for melting snow or making ice cream. Place the rock salt in a coffee can or a container which has a lid and is big enough so you can shake the rock salt thoroughly.

In a measuring cup place a teaspoon of water. Add twenty drops of food coloring to the water and mix well. You can color the rock salt according to the following color scheme. Use red food color for love, vitality or rejuvenation. Use blue for calm, tranquility, and peace. Use green for health or healing—you should advise the person to see a physician as well. Use yellow for mental stimulation. Combine fifteen drops of yellow and five drops of red for prosperity or success in business.

Add whatever herbs or perfumes you wish to add, finely ground, to the measuring cup, and mix up again. Now add the contents of the measuring cup to the rock salt. Place the lid on the rock salt can and shake it thoroughly. If you mix it well you will have a nice even color all over the salt crystals. If desired, you can dry the salt before using it. It should have a fairly uniform color, with bits of the herbs sticking to some of the rock salt crystals.

I use a half teaspoon of ground cloves in the red rock salt, a half teaspoon of ground rosemary in the green rock salt, and a quarter teaspoon of mint in the yellow rock salt. I like to add a teaspoon of epsom salt to the rock salt before mixing it. It is also possible to add baking soda if you desire to raise the vibration of the mixture a bit.

THE OBI STICK, OR STAFF OF HERMES

The Obi stick, or caduceus, or staff of Hermes, as it is variously known, is an emblem of power and the control of power. It is a "magic wand" in the literal sense, and specifically signifies the ability of its user to control the universal life force. It is thus a potent tool for an aspiring magician or witch to prepare. Its obvious use requires no explanation, as those who cannot immediately think of uses will probably not be able to use it in any event.

The method used to prepare one of these wands is the best kept secret of the various practices which use them. In the Obeah practice of Jamaica, the secret of the Obi stick is very carefully protected, so much so that most of the better practitioners will only make one to hand on their power to a successor. That a chicken is sacrificed to the tree which gives its wood for the Obi stick is only the beginning of a long and complicated ritual by which the stick is made.

Many years ago when I lived in a back country area, I had occasion to make two or three of these wands for students. I made them according to the following method, and as they were well received and put to good use I have no hesitation in recommending the method, although, so far as I know, it comes from no practice of which I have received formal training or informal knowledge. As the method requires access to a "wild place," preferably deep in the woods, it is unlikely that many people will be able to follow the directions given. These arts are more for the country person than the city dweller.

The finished wands have a very good feel, and once they are consecrated they may be put to good use. I have even had a Jamaican Obi man ask me how I had made such a powerful stick! The ritual of producing the wand takes a long time, but the result is well worth the effort.

Firstly, enter the wild place and find a young oak tree, or a swamp oak. Locate two good ivy vines, in the same area if possible. Make friends with the young oak tree, and get its permission to become a wand. This usually takes several weeks of conversation and discussion with the spirit of the tree. Unless the tree is immediately willing to become a wand, it's worth spending some time with the tree discussing just what you have in mind for the wand. The time will not be wasted in any event. I have had a tree point out that the wands I was looking for were in process of being naturally made only a few feet away from where we had been talking.

The tree, once it has given permission to be made into a wand, should be watered with a solution made of a half cup blood meal, a quarter cup of bone meal, and a cup of good nitrogen fertilizer to about three gallons of water. This should be done in the fall of the year, after the autumnal equinox. This is the usual price for the wood, and it is better than sacrificing a chicken as the fertilizer will go right to work, while the chicken would have to decompose.

The following year, about Candlemas, visit the tree again, and find the branch you desire. It should be a fairly low main branch about an inch in diameter, although a three-fourths inch diameter is all right. Transplant some ivy vines to the base of the oak as soon as possible, and cover the area around the base of the tree with small pebbles to keep bush growth away from the tree and the vines.

After the vernal equinox, or as soon as the ivy vines are established, tie the vines to train them to the oak. You want to get the vines to your branch as directly as possible. At this time you may want to prune the tree, being careful to discuss this with the tree in advance. Prune just enough to eliminate suckers and dead wood.

By midsummer the vines should be at your branch, and well-trained to the tree. Twist the vines around the branch to form a helix (or spiral), and tie them in place if necessary. The vines must be tight to the branch.

From this point on you must check the tree every month or so. Keep the vines tight to the bark of the branch, the excess vine and tree well cut back, and the vine and the tree healthy and well-contented. This process continues for two or three years.

In time the vines will strangle the branch in the pattern of the helix, and there will be a definite marriage of the two in the process. Once the branch is about an inch and a quarter in diameter at its smallest end, and the vine from a quarter to three-eighths inch in diameter, the branch and vines are ready to be cut out.

The permission of the tree must be obtained again, and the vines should also be told that their purpose is at an end. The actual cutting should take place between the autumnal equinox and the winter solstice. First the growth end of the vine should be cut, and then the growing end. Then the vines themself, which hopefully you have kept from spreading, should be uprooted and cast from the tree to ensure that the tree will not be strangled by the vine after it has yielded the wand.

The growing end of the branch is now severed from the tree's main trunk and your branch is at hand. The wound on the tree should be dressed, covered, and patched so the tree will not rot. It may be necessary to warm pitch for this purpose. All trimming of the tree should be done at once, and the pruning of the tree also done to remove suckers and dead wood. The object is to leave the tree in as healthy a condition as possible.

The finished branch should be between three and four feet long, with the two helical vines which have impressed themselves into the bark of the branch for about half their diameter. As mentioned, all the cuttings of the branch and the tree prunings should be left at the base of the tree. The tree should be thanked for giving you the branch.

The trimmed branch must then be dried for a while, at least until the vernal equinox, before it is worked for use. If it is desired to glue the vines to the branch – a wise idea – either fish glue or hoof glue should be used. Casine or plastic glues will change the feel of the wand. The glueing should be done before the consecration, which may be done according to any method you prefer.

READING LIST

The following books are either referred to in the text, or they contain useful material which expands on the text.

Psychic Protection and Removal of Psychic Influences

Psychic Self Defense by Dion Fortune
First printed in 1930, this work has been reprinted a number of times. It is usually the first book a novice magician is told to purchase. Published by Aquarian Press, Wellingborough, England and distributed in the USA by Samuel Weiser, York Beach, ME.

Spiritual Cleansing by Draja Mickaharic
Published in 1982 by Samuel Weiser, York Beach, ME. This work deals with the removal of negative spiritual influences. I wrote this book for the layperson rather than the novice magician (the audience for Dion Fortune's work).

Spiritual Properties of the Plant, Animal, and Mineral World

The Psychic Garden by Mellie Uyldert
Published by Thorsons Publishing Group, Wellingborough, England, 1980.

Metal Magic by Mellie Uyldert
Published by Thorsons Publishing Group, Wellingborough, England, 1980.

The Magic of Precious Stones by Mellie Uyldert
Published by Thorsons Publishing Group, Wellingborough, England, 1981.
The author of these three books is a brilliant and understanding psychic whose primary interest is healing. All three of these books are the best in their field! The English editions are translated from the original Dutch.

Living Medicine by Mannfried Pahlow
Published by Thorsons Publishing Group, Wellingborough, England, 1980.
This book deals entirely with herbal healing, but it is worth reading because it gives a very complete introduction to the anatomy of plants. Acquaintanceship with the book will build the necessary understanding of the plant kingdom which one must have in order to work with the herbs magically. Translated from the German.

Herbs

The following herbal references are a good starting point for exploring the vegetable kingdom, whether for healing or for magical use.

The Herb Book by John Lust
Available from Benedict Lust Publications, 490 Easy Street, Simi Valley, CA 93065.

Back to Eden by Jethro Kloss
Back to Eden Book, Loma Linda, CA. Also available from Benedict Lust Publications.

Magical Practices

Most books about magical practices are not written by those who are initiates of the practice. All of the books listed here are written by initiates in the practice of which they write.

Natural Magic by Doreen Valiente
Phoenix Publishing, Custer, WA, 1985.

Positive Magic by Marion Weinstein
Phoenix Publishing, Custer, WA, 1981

Santeria: African Magic in Latin America by Migene Gonzalez-Wippler, Original Publications, NY, 1976.

Strange Experience by Lee R. Gandee, Prentice-Hall, Englewood Cliffs, NJ, 1971.

Magic and Spells

The Book of Secrets of Alburtus Magnus
Of the Virtues of Herbs, Stones and Certain Beasts;
also a Book of the Marvels of the World
Edited by Michael R. Best and Frank H. Brightman
Published by Oxford University Press, NY, 1973, paper edition, 1974.
This is the best edition of *Alburtus Magnus,* but it is likely to be difficult to find. It reveals what our ancestors believed in, and can teach us that beliefs are a variable thing.

The Archidoxes of Magic by Paracelsus
Published by Samuel Weiser, York Beach, ME, 1975, now out-of-print.
This is a facsimile of the first English edition of 1656. While it makes interesting reading, it is another guide to ancient beliefs. There are some excellent points in it, however, which make it worth reading.

Pow-Wows or the Long Lost Friend by John George Hohman
Published by Fulton Religious Supply Co., NY.
There are better editions of this book available, but they are
hard to find. The work was first published in the 1820's and
has been kept in print since then. This alone is a good testimony to its usefulness!

INDEX

A

B